Shenanigans The History of QPR's Casuals

Dave Cas

Back cover image courtesy of and thanks to Ian Podevin

Book cover designed by Rebecacovers, Fiverr.com

ISBN: 9798746406750

DEDICATION

For anyone who grew up in the late 1970's and early 1980's and followed their football club around the country.
This is dedicated to a good friend George who recently passed away, we had some good times supporting our Queens Park Rangers FC.
Also RIP Jon Jon and big Streatham Steve staunch QPR lads and funny as they come.
For all R's supporters and all of you just reminiscing about the past.

CONTENTS

ACKNOWLEDGMENTS

Thanks to everyone who contributed with your memories and stories. No need to mention your names.

1 THE BEGINNING

As I write this book, I am fifty three years old and am living in Donegal, Ireland about as far away from West London as I could be.

I grew up in South West London, Teddington to be exact and then in Hanworth. My upbringing was terrible, those that know me know.

I am not going into details about that but I did write my first book "Beating My Demons" all about that and my life.

Probably everyone has their own "demons," shit happens and is always happening.

I was bought up amid drunken violence and guess what that's exactly what I became involved in. The horrors of my childhood did not deter me from becoming what I saw. So it took thirty seven years for me to realize what I was doing wasn't right.

The first fight I ever had in my life was when I beat up the fella that was trying to bully me at school. I got a proper buzz from that and then I became accepted and I felt like I was "somebody".

That was about 1980, we all know what happened in the 1980's, football hooliganism was rife and it was also part of being a "casual". Or maybe it wasn't for some casuals who were literally in it just for the fashion.

I was a punk, then a skinhead and then became a dresser or casual. It was smart being a casual, and there was tens or even hundreds of thousands of other lads doing just the same.

I started to support QPR at the age of eight years old, which coincided with the R's best ever league season finishing second in the old First Division (now the Premier League).

So why am I writing this book? Maybe it is a follow on from my second book "MemoiR's" This is about supporting QPR and a lot of memories and opinions from fellow fans of my favourite team.

This book is going to be about memories and reminiscing of the past. For me it will never be again, I am a self-confessed alcoholic who got sober more than fifteen years ago.

The booze had a massive impact on my behaviour and who I was and the way I perceived the world. I am different now especially in my thinking.

Throughout the years I had four banning orders from football and a couple of small stints inside. I also served several sentences for robbing clothes shops and other drunken fighting.

My last ban was in 2004 which coincided with me getting sober. I knocked all the aggro lark on the head then and it is certainly not worth all the consequences again.

I would suggest to any lad reading this book to not bother getting involved end of story.

This is all about memories and the past. I am not condoning or glorifying football violence in any way. As I have written two books already, I now have the bug for being an author!

There have been books on many clubs firms and not one

about QPR. So basically I am just the author, don't shoot the messenger!

Football hooliganism in the 1980s was in some way "fashionable" admittedly not the best way to be going about it but was just a part of history. The hooligan books are a "genre" of their own. And as I have a massive love for my team Queens Park Rangers, I am writing this book for keepsake purposes.

Other authors have written about mass murderers, true crime, government scandals and such like. The general public love reading about these things, and are genuinely interested. So why not write a book about QPR's lads and all the shenanigans?

My first ever time I witnessed any kind of trouble at football was at Crystal Palace v Cardiff. My mum had a friend whose daughters took me along to Palace, that's who they supported. This was before I had even been to a QPR match.

A lot of my attention was focused on the Cardiff fans, only a few hundred of them were behind the goal in the end where the Sainsbury's is now at Selhurst Park.

They must have been well pissed up because it was like they were "mad" throughout the whole match. Palace won 2-0 and even though they were losing the Welshmen kept on singing and hurling abuse at the South Londoners. They were very loyal to their club and totally out-sang the Palace lot.

Anyway, as the girls led us back to the motor after the final whistle; it was winter and the skies were dark already. We walked hastily along the pavement and about ten minutes later a couple of coaches came slowly past us.

All of a sudden there was a loud crashing noise and glass was shattering all over the road. The nutty Cardiff fans had smashed the windows of their coach from inside and were throwing anything they could at the Palace fans walking along.

I was only about seven or eight years old and I kind of froze on the spot, one of the girls grabbed my arm and marched us off as quickly as we could.

"Don't worry about them, they are just a bunch of animals" and then we were out of sight.

To be honest I was quite scared by that incident but at the

same time it was exciting in a crazy kind of way.

I attended my first ever match at Loftus Road the home of my beloved Queens Park Rangers in the season of 1977/78. My mum's boyfriend Patrick who was an Irishman and an ex rugby player himself. I don't think he even liked football but I think my mum gave so much grief about taking me he literally had to.

Patrick took us to one night match and we went in the school end terrace behind the goal. This was a vast old end which was really for the away fans. I believe it was cheaper to get in there than the Loft. Patrick either took me in there to save money or just out of pure spite.

Anyway that first game under the lights was a memory I will never forget. We lost the game 3-1 and what grabbed my attention that night was the huge defender for Wolves, his name was Bob Hazell and he later went on to sign for us. Big Bob played in the FA cup Final in 81/2 versus Tottenham. It was in those early 80's that the racial riots started in Brixton and there was disorder in Wolverhampton. It was on the news that Bob had been nicked for siphoning petrol out of motors. What a chap!

My first away game following my team couldn't have been any better. It was at the Bridge home of Chelsea or the "scum" as they are affectionately known by many of the QPR faithful. They are our hated neighbours, I know most Chelsea heads say they couldn't give a toss about us. But like it or not there has been a rivalry between us.

Admittedly in the 60's through to around the late 80's Chelsea turned up in their masses at Loftus Road and literally took over. There were the odd skirmishes when die hard rangers lads tried to protect our territory but it never really ended well. It wasn't really until the 1990's that we started to stand up for ourselves against the scum.

It was around 1980 that I saw the first aggro at a QPR match, this is when myself and my pal Martin had started to go on our own to the games.

And it was against, yes you guessed it Cardiff! What was it about Cardiff? And at that time I had not put two and two together.

Myself and Martin used to go in the Loft, up behind the goal at the back, probably not the best view but we loved the atmosphere and all the banter we heard from the older lads that congregated there.

When you are just a young teenager you kind of look up to the elders as folk heroes, well I did anyway! QPR have always had some weird and wonderful characters, which makes the whole match experience all the more entertaining.

Now this particular game was another 2-0 loss for the boys from the Valleys and a win for mighty R's. Clive Allen probably scored, as he always did around that time.

I was a skinhead by this time and Martin was a punk with his spiky hair and mohair jumper and black leather jacket. I wore a sheepskin coat too big for me as I had nicked it from Patrick, and a lot of skins were wearing them at the time. Many older lads wore the old donkey jackets, I think I did own one for a while but to be honest I much preferred the sheepskin complete with glue stains from our sniffing adventures!

The game had only been going about ten minutes when two geezers out of the blue started going ballistic. They were waving their arms about like windmills and trying to hit anyone in their sight.

There was no way me and Martin could do anything, these fellas were way older than us and they looked like coal miners built like brick shit-houses!

It was all over in seconds as they were both nabbed by the old bill who marched them off in arm locks. I think they took a few sly kicks as they were herded through the terrace.

That made for a very hostile atmosphere after that and had stoked up the lads in the Loft to sing ant-Welsh songs for the rest of the match. Cardiff had quite a few in the away end that day, but the talk was all about retribution following the game.

At the end of the match all the older lot seemed to be gathering at the exit in a big mob, so out of excitement we followed them to see what was going to occur.

Anyone that has been involved in any trouble will know of that feeling in the stomach, like adrenaline flowing through the body. It is a mix of fear and anticipation, kind of like going on a white knuckle ride at a fun fair.

Now, when you come out of the Loft into Loftus Road, it is lined with terraced houses and off to the left there is a grassy square with blocks of flats on both sides. The

Springbok pub backed on to the square which led to South Africa Road. All along SA Road is the White City estate. It is huge and had rows and rows with the old style tenement blocks with the open walkways.

To the left of the Springbok is a line of shops which back in those days would have been a newsagent, bookies and a chip shop, possibly there was a launderette as well.

This is where the trouble started right by the shops, there was fights breaking out all over the place. It looked as though the coppers had ran off up SA Road where obviously there was more trouble kicking off.

We saw one bloke getting floored by a solid right hander, when he landed on the deck someone threw a house brick which cracked the poor fellas head. At the time I didn't know whether to be shocked or amused by this scene!

After that, myself and Martin decided to leave the vicinity and head back down Loftus Road and get back to public transport to take us home.

We spoke about this most of the way home and I believe this is where it cemented my interest in the fighting at football. Like I said earlier I had no direction in my life, all I saw was drinking and violence indoors from my mother. Maybe this was my way of venting out all the hurt and frustration that I was experiencing myself.

My biggest passion was just supporting QPR, and in only my second season of watching them we were relegated from the old Division One to the second Division.

Under our manager Terry Venables we got a plastic pitch, it was a bit like Marmite, either love it or hate it!

To be honest I only liked it and defended it against all the mockers because we did well on it. We got to the FA Cup final in 1982 and played Spurs. We lost the replay, I was only fourteen years old at the time but have heard over the years there was a fair bit of trouble at both those games.

The only sort of violence I witnessed was when my mates' dad was walking us back to his Sherpa Van to take us all home. We must have been walking along the North Circular Road and we were by a fly-over. The traffic lights went red ahead and a car load of Spurs fans stopped at the lights. They were all giving it out of the windows taking the piss out of the rangers fans walking along.

That was like waving a red flag to a pack of bulls, because

four or five QPR lads pulled every one of them except the driver out of the motor. They got a right kicking and were all laid out like skittles and the driver sped off into the distance leaving his wounded pals behind.

Myself and Mart found this hilarious, that would teach them! As a young tear-away it gave me a sense of pride that our own fans had got retribution.

The next season 1982/83 was my favourite of all time supporting the R's. I was now getting old enough to start going to away games on my own with Mart. My mum had been in and out of psychiatric hospital and my home life was horrendous, pure drunkenness and the things I witnessed were horrible.

I was an angry kid and going to football was my outlet and the only place I felt alive and part of something.

So back to the football I don't want to bore anyone with that shit, but I feel it is relevant as to why I started to do what I did.

QPR were playing well in 82/3 we were up the top of the table and I went to as many games as I could and that included away games. I had to beg my mum for money and if she didn't give me any I would nick the odd fiver out of her purse. Anyway that would be a fiver less she could spend on the booze.

Back in those days it was only a few quid to get in to the games and we used to go on the "special" train to the away games, which were subsidized by the club. We used to go in the Sherpa Van earlier in the season to places like Barnsley, Rotherham, Cambridge and even Wolves away.

Then we started venturing out and get on the special trains. It was on one of those specials that I started to become part of the mob at the rangers. I was only fifteen, so it would have been like being one of the "youth" that clubs have these days. Only in those days the youth mixed with the older geezers. We were "tag- alongs" and made up the numbers, QPR's away support was nothing like Chelsea or the bigger teams of the day. That didn't matter in some ways it was a closer knit feel about it because everyone knew each other by face and there was a sense of loyalty like no other.

A game changer for me was when we played Leeds away in 82/83, as usual me and Mart went up on the "special" that day. A lot of the older lot had gone to this on that train as well probably because it was cheap. I believe our chairman of the time subsidized a lot of away trips that season.

Everyone knew about Leeds reputation, it was around the time that the Service Crew were in the news and were causing mayhem! This away trip wasn't for the feint hearted, a lot like going to the Old Den or Ayresome Park (I never went there).

To be fair we had a decent turn out that day by our standards. And being in the company of the C-Mob was a buzz for us youngsters.

I don't really remember much about the match or the whole day, but what stands out for me forever is the trip back on the train.

I was still a skinhead at this time and I wore a shabby old sheepskin coat which was covered in glue stains from my glue sniffing sessions!

About twenty or so of the C Mob came marching through our carriage and as we sat there all excited about our 1-0 win; one of the oldest lads said to me and Mart "You are good lads, but you need to smarten yourselves up".

I could of taken that as a right insult and could have gone home sulking. Instead I took it on the chin and decided there and then that I was going to shape up or ship out.

When we got back to London, it was either St. Pancras or Kings Cross there was that sense of proudness when we all got off the train in a large group. Anyone who remembers the 80's will remember the football "bowl" the cocky strutting and walking along with arms swinging like a small army marching along.

As we came off the platform and toward one of the stairways down to the underground a roar went up and the older boys all steamed out of the exit. There had been a little firm of Gooners outside we found out later. I am not 100 % sure what happened but apparently C-Mob did well.

In the 1980's and even to a certain extent these days there will always be different mobs floating around. The exciting part of that was you never knew who we were going to bump into.

The Casual/ dresser scene was taking off and all the firms that were wearing all the clobber really looked the part. It was all diamond cut Pringles, Ellesse, Fila and Taccini tracksuit tops. The Service Crew were notorious for wearing deer stalker hats and some of our boys wore them too.

So the first items of attire that I managed to get my hands on were a plain yellow Pringle jumper, a Patrick wind cheater coat and a deer stalker. I had those white strap-over trainers, there was no way I could afford the Trim Trabb or Forest Hills.

Wearing the gear did wonders for my confidence, as I said before my home life and family were fucked right up.

This is what a Rotherham lad had to say about the early days of dressers from QPR;

"I was around thirteen years old when I went to Millmoor to watch Rotherham v QPR. It was an entertaining action packed game with three sendings off, one for Rotherham two for QPR. The then manager Terry Venables was sent to the stands. Anyway when Rotherham kicked towards the away end, me and a few mates would switch towards that section to be closer to any goals we would score. On this action packed day I saw something I had never seen before, a decent size mob of away fans slightly distanced from the scarf wearers and shirt wearers. They all looked like they could be brothers with the same wedge mushroom haircuts and diamond jumpers, kagools, bleached jeans and white trainers. My mate who was a year older than me said he had seen some photos in a magazine, they are called trendies. I kept watching between the action and they looked different to any other mobs of away fans I had seen. They were smart and clean looking and had a certain swagger and the local plod seemed to gather in big numbers close to them. It was probably at least eighteen months later when it would catch on in Rotherham, mind you they did have Stuarts on their doorstep. Nearly forty years later and the style is still going strong to the chosen few. Respect. "DP" Rotherham".

Stuarts was an excellent shop on the Uxbridge Road and funnily enough owned by a geezer called Stiart! It had all the latest clobber. Lads from all over London and across the UK would visit this gaff.

"Taxing" was rife in those days, that was clothing being taken off someone, usually at knife point. A lot of that went on around Stuarts.

Another memorable night from that season was at Charlton, they still had that massive terrace at the side in those days. If I remember rightly the away stand was being re-built so we were standing on the opposite side to that huge steep terrace.

There must have been a mob of our fans in there as I could see a running battle ensuing all the way along which resulted in the Charlton lot being run back into their end behind the goal. It was strange because there were no police to be seen and it was like they were all left to just get on with it!

The rest of the 82/83 season was blinding, we went up as Champions and the last three home games were very memorable to say the least. We played Leeds, Fulham and Wolves and obviously all those teams bought big mobs and filled the away end.

After the Leeds game I saw a load of them get caught up in the White City estate, there was no escape for them they took a right kicking. I am not sure about any other main events that day but I am sure there were loads!

I have heard from many of ours and Fulham's chaps that there were offs all day and again after the match I followed on with one of the biggest mobs of rangers I have ever seen.

That firm we had that day was also the best dressed lot I have ever seen down at the R's. Carrying umbrellas seemed to be a thing at the time, and would be used as a cosh if needed.

We marched from the Bush all the way down to Hammersmith Broadway. All the boys were saying to keep going down Fulham Palace Road and to Fulham's manor. The old bill was in force at the Broadway and stopped us from going any further.

Then came the Wolves game, fair play they bought loads and at the final whistle we invaded the pitch in celebration of winning the Division and being promoted to the top flight.

There was several punch ups occurring all round the away end and the wall at the bottom of the Ellerslie Road stand collapsed with a surge of fans, luckily no one was hurt.

A Wolves lad said this on facebook; "Some of us Wolves lads were in the seats to the right of the away stand, it went mental at the end on the pitch in the corner and in the seats. QPR fans came at us from everywhere. Great days, and great memories."

The last away game of that season was at Grimsby, and we were already Champions so took a massive following up there. A lot of the older boys and C-Mob went up on the Friday night and there are plenty of stories to be told there.

Me and Mart went up on the Special, we didn't personally see any rows but there was all day apparently. Apparently there was one big off down some side streets where it was full on and there were lumps of wood, bricks, bottles and other weaponry emptied from a skip being used.

The following are events written by mates, this one is from Kev:

Grimsby Away 1982/83. QPR were top of division two, promotion fever was in the air so off we went to Grimsby to party. We left in a mini bus at 8 am on the Friday for Cleethorpes, a stone's throw from the ground. We stopped off in Nottingham for a few pints on the way then off to the coast. After booking in to B and B's and a couple of pints in a little pub we set off for somewhere livelier, We found a big gaff called The Dolphin which had four or five bars and a disco (nightclub if you're under fifty). After a few hours sampling the different bars and trying it on with the local talent we were a bit spread out over the complex. Four of us were standing at the bar when Dave the Para came running in "Keith’s outside having a ruck " we ran out the front door, no sign of Keith so we turned left and then left again, still no sign. We were nearly back where we started in a large dark car park. Shouting made us turn & look up a narrow entrance to the car park and there he was, good old Keith, arms swinging legs swinging holding back probably nine or ten locals. It was hard to tell it was so dark! Keith had probably been at it for a few minutes now which was quite impressive! That's a long time to be on your own against those odds. “C'mon” we yelled as we went to his aid, now I don't know what they thought but I'd be thinking we can't beat one on his own now he's got five mates with him, bollocks to this! So obviously they turned and legged it, we gave chase onto the seafront, unlucky for the four we caught up with, they were pretty big lads, which made Keith’s one man stand even more impressive! When we got back to the bars pub me and Keith went to the gents to clean him up a bit just a few little scratches and bumps, nothing serious although he did look very pale now the adrenaline rush had stopped. We headed back to the bars to be greeted by the sound of fighting and breaking glass. The rest of the lads were in a fight in one of the bars, little

Pete was in the doorway and it was all kicking off " I think N has just glassed one of them " I told Keith to stay where he was because he hadn't quite recovered yet and went in. But by now it was practically over, the bouncers had separated the two groups! We decided not to push our luck & move on to another pub, there had been no sign of dibble yet (found out later that we weren't the only rangers in town and they had their hands full elswhere). The rest of the night was a much quieter affair although we did have a minor skirmish on the way back to the digs. We used to do the Friday night thing three or four times a season in the 70s & 80s we just loved the rush of being in someone else's town!

On the Saturday we had breakfast followed by a few beers in Cleethorpes, we bumped into a few more R's who told us of stabbings and smashed pubs the night before, how much of it was true or Chinese whispers I don't know. That day the only trouble I saw was when a dozen or so Grimsby near the ground started pavement dancing and Scrappy (actually a Brentford fan along for the crack) went over and slapped one and got nicked for it! Rangers did the business and we all got soaked in some of the heaviest rain I've ever seen.

From a Grimsby lad; "Grimsby had a good off with you at our ground in the early 80s, went off down a side street and there was a skip full of wood with both mobs toe to toe and planks of wood across a few heads."

" After the game we all walked back to the mini bus like we ruled the place all untouchable. But our stop off in Lincoln on the way back was to prove otherwise!

We got back to our minibus after the game, across the road we saw another one and realized my mate Paul and his brother Billy were in the front. After a brief chat we decided to join up and have a couple of pints in Lincoln to break up the journey home. Our two minibuses arrived in Lincoln about an hour later, we got out and the two groups had the usual chat about their experiences of the day. The town was pretty quiet, that time in between shoppers and night time drinkers! It took about five minutes to find a likely bar, as we walked in it looked like we had the place to ourselves. It was large with a balcony overlooking a dance floor below. I couldn't resist a peek over. As I looked down I saw six men sitting next to the empty dance floor staring back up at me expressionless! The bar staff refused to serve us because we were too large a group. After a bit of grumbling and trying to convince them we were students we decided on another pub 200 yards down the road. We got served with no problem, probably glad of the trade as it was a bit of a dive! I drunk about half my beer and decided I needed food, so set off by myself to find a chippy which took about five minutes. After eating my pie and chips I headed back to the pub to wash them down. I could hear the noise and guess what was happening before I saw it. As I turned the corner there it was the pub was under siege! How was I going to get back in? There were thirty or more of the biggest ugliest blokes I'd ever seen trying to get in. A few police were there trying to hold them back, one massive copper, shaved head and helmet discarded was having a toe to toe with an equally massive local like two bare knuckle fighters.

I wandered up as casually as I could saw a gap and dived into the door as I did someone whacked me in the side of the head, the hardest hit I'd taken all weekend was from another QPR fan who got a bit over excited! I'd recognized some of the locals as those downstairs in the other bar. The barman had told some of the others that this was a regular occurrence those locals outside weren't football fans just chaps who expected anyone playing Grimsby to stop off in Lincoln. Some of the lads put pool balls in socks ready to charge out, a piece of wood smashed through the window showering us with glass. That was it we charged out of the door ready to chase them off and show them who was the boss! Unfortunately it didn't work out that way as we went at them they came back at us, we had an ex Para, at least two boxers and enough handy lads to stand against most, but this lot to be honest were bigger, uglier and angrier than us ,we were being pushed back towards the doorway, fighting but not well enough, we started falling over each other going backwards, fighting but getting beaten, enough was enough, most of us had already been pushed back into the pub and the rest of us decided it was time to join them. Thankfully nobody was too badly hurt physically but our pride had taken a battering, twenty four hours earlier we thought nobody could touch us, well those Lincoln lads taught us otherwise! I've read books where some firms never lose a fight, that's just bollocks! We all get a spanking occasionally or in my case quite a lot!

Before I go into Chapter two "The 80's", I would like to reiterate that QPR were by no means a big player in the football hooligan scene. We held our own and stung many a big team at home and did more than enough at the smaller teams away.

We were not in the same league as the Chelsea's, Millwalls and West Hams, although we did ok against Spurs at home and the odd time against Arsenal.

2 THE 80'S

The following season 1983/84 was our first back in the top division since we were relegated in 1979. Our first home game was against Aston Villa and I remember standing in the Paddock that day. The paddock was and still is the lower tier of the South Africa Road stand.

Just before the game had even kicked of there was a bit of trouble up in the top tier of the away end. About twenty older lads were having a good ding dong of a row up by one of the entrances. It took old bill a while to break it all up, but that had set the scene for the rest of the season.

For me football was all about meeting up with your mates whether it was at home or away and having a good laugh. The 1980's was an era when looking smart was part and parcel of being a casual football lad.

It was a great feeling especially at other towns and cities when a big group (or even small on some occasions!) got off the train and walked through the exit into the unknown.

As the train pulled in to our destination I would get that feeling of excitement in the stomach. There was always that possibility of getting ambushed on the way out or the anticipation of what could happen throughout the day.

Back in the 80's we would arrive early enough to not have a big old bill welcoming committee waiting for us. We would march in and find a boozer to settle for the day. Sometimes there would be a pub right by the station and we would go in there only if we felt there was not enough of us to venture in to town centres where it came on top quite quickly. Certain places would be a no go and QPR would not even attempt to blatantly make a show.

There was now a small group of us who used to go on the service trains, a few lads from Feltham, and a mix from the Bush, Edgware Road and Hayes. We would always meet up later on with all the other lot that came up with Gregor and co. Gregor would always rally the troops and made it clear that anyone who ran that day would be dealt with on the journey home!

The C-Mob who I will go into later mainly did their own thing and fair play to them.

QPR have always had loads of different mobs, there was the Bush lot, the Grove lot and those two often didn't see eye to eye. At the Milk Cup final in 87 at Wembley I heard it got nasty in the ground between them. The fact that we got smashed 3-0 by Oxford probably set the scene for everyone getting the right hump. I was nicked before that game which in an ironic way saved me the misery of watching that match.

I was only sixteen and most of my interest was getting pissed and hopefully getting into a punch up. I do not claim to be a top boy or anything like that, I was just another Joe Bloggs who stuck with my mates and we all looked out for each other. I was game though and when I had a good session on the Stella I had no fear. I would always try and be at the front when it went off. I didn't care if I took a good clump but luckily enough I never took a bad bashing at football in those days.

There was certain games where trouble would be guaranteed and for us that was at Norwich, Ipswich, Luton, Oxford, Nottm Forest, Watford, Southampton and of course the London Derbies. Nothing major happened at the big teams, although there would always be some kind of small off somewhere. It was mainly at home as we had to defend our territory.

As I started to get a bit older in my mid teens I got into more punch ups, and that is all they were really. Every weekend I would get into some drunken brawl in my local pubs and football was just the excuse I needed to have a row with someone. I had no fear to be honest and found it a proper buzz running into another mob even when we were outnumbered. I did not really have a care for my own safety, a kind of self-harm!

Here are a few stories from the 80s in no particular order;

Crystal Palace Home. 1981/82 FA Cup QF. There had been quite a bit of trouble between us in recent matches home and away. This one was very spicy as we now had Terry Venables their ex-manager and Clive Allen who played for them. The ground was packed to the rafters and the atmosphere was intense and hostile. I was only fourteen and with my best pal as always. Clive Allen popped in the winner in the last minute and ran toward the Palace end giving them the V-sign! To say the South London lot went berserk in an understatement. Fans from both ends steamed toward each other and it was going off all over the place. This is a comment left on the youtube clip of the Big Match highlights; "Shame they didn't show the seven police horses come on the pitch to separate five hundred fans fighting .Was funny when Allen scored and a Palace fan chased him and tried to kick him up the ass". Outside was mayhem everywhere, and it was hard to tell who was who. This was the beginning of the dresser era and most lads were wearing Pringles etc. From what I saw there was no real winner here just pure fighting everywhere which went on for hours after.

Norwich Away 1. About twenty of us got up there early and went in a pub right by the station. We waited there for all the others to arrive. Word must have got out that we were there and all of a sudden there was a roar from around forty of them outside. There was a huge car park filled with cars in front of the pub and station. We just grabbed as many bottles from the tables as we could and charged out of the front door. Norwich backed off and ran through the car park at the same time as chucking bricks and bottles back at us. A bit later on we headed to another pub by a canal and it began filling up with loads of us QPR. About an hour before kick off Gregor came running in announcing that Norwich were down in the market square. Virtually the whole pub emptied out and we ran down this steep hill, a few Norwich stood and got slapped and the rest were gone. After the match there was skirmishes all the way back to the station.

Norwich Away 2. I went up with about a dozen of us, it was our usual crowd, I won't mention any names. It was the usual drinking before the match and we decided to get seat tickets in the upper tier of the Norwich end. We won 2-0 and we celebrated each goal, the locals were not happy! At the end of the match virtually the whole end turned on us, my jeans were ripped clambering over the seats to get out. I was gutted they were faded Lois jeans I had just saved up for and now my arse was hanging out the back due to the big tear. As we left the ground we had to run to get away from the hundreds of Norwich frothing at the mouth. We made it back to the away end in one piece and re-joined our fellows for the long walk back to the station. As always at Norwich, there were small running battles and toe to toes everywhere.

Norwich Away 3. As with other times at Norwich we had a decent turnout up there. Nothing happened before the match but the walk back to the station was very eventful. Myself and half a dozen of my mates broke away from the rest and as we neared the station I ended up running into four Norwich lads and put one of them on his arse. The old bill saw what happened and I tried to avoid them. While this was going on the main lot of rangers were having a massive stand-off on the adjacent road. Around that time a gooner lad from Ladbroke Grove used to come with us for the laugh. He was a massive lad and was called Mr T for obvious reasons. I saw him wrench a concrete bollard out of the pavement and toss it like a caber at the Norwich fans. It was like he was having his own Highland games!

Another toe to toe ensued and I had to fend off a couple of Norwich lads running in to me. I was nabbed by a copper who grabbed me by the scruff of the neck and he escorted me back to the station. He told me to get on the next train home or I would be nicked.

In those days in the early 80's it was good to get a smack from a copper rather than get nicked. It was only in later years that nickings became more frequent and sentences got tougher. I believe that the use of Stanley knives started to make football hooliganism a lot more sinister.

Ipswich Away 1. I went up with my usual crowd, and this time I took my mate Joe an Arsenal fan and nutter himself. He was interested to see if QPR were as good as I said they were at the time! Nothing much happened before the game but as we came out we had a good hundred or so main lot including lads from the C-Mob.

The old bill had us in an escort and as we went further, a big mob of Ipswich came toward us from the road in front of us. Back in the 80s there was like a war cry that went up and everyone steamed through the police. Ipswich ran to the left and all the way round a big area of derelict grounds which was fenced off. It was the size of a big football pitch. We all ran the opposite way round and we collided straight into the Ipswich half way round. We definitely had the better of things and old bill gathered us all back up and back to the station.

Ipswich Away 2. This was the Milk Cup Quarter Final I think maybe 1985. The weather had been terrible and the game had already been postponed twice. We all used to drink in the Princess Vic down the Uxbridge Road in those days.

Coaches had been arranged from the pub and there was a good 150 of just from that one pub. It was a right downer when the game was called off at the last minute, at least it was postponed before we left for Ipswich! I thought there was no way that all this lot would turn up a third time, but fair play we did.

For some reason our coaches ended up in a side terrace meant for home fans. It was a shit match, 0-0 if I remember correctly. At the final whistle, Ipswich on the side opposite us obviously had the hump that we were in their end and they began coming at us over the pitch. They had picked up the advertising hoardings and were hurling them at us like missiles. There were toe to toes and running battles on the pitch for what seemed like ages. Eventually the pitch was cleared and as we left the ground the lot I was with charged a load of Ipswich down the road. A few of ours were banged up for that incident.

This was the write up in the East Anglian Times, 24th January 1985. Rival fans battled on the pitch at the end of the Milk Cup Quarter Final goaless draw between Ipswich Town and Queens Park Rangers. Police say that about eighteen arrests were made and that three people were taken to the Heath

Road Wing of Ipswich Hospital. Further details were not immediately available. Helmets were sent flying as police waded in to separate the rival factions. At one stage fights were going on all over the field. Policemen were hard pressed to prevent a large gang of Londoners from attacking a smaller group of Ipswich troublemakers who had invaded the pitch. Trouble had begun early in the second half soon after a can had been thrown on to the pitch from the side stand where the visiting fans were in great numbers. Police from all sections of the ground rushed to the corner and pulled out visiting supporters who fought as they were led away. As the final whistle sounded, fans poured on to the pitch from all directions testing the police presence to the limit. It was one of the worse after match incidents at Portman Road. Ipswich manager Bobby Ferguson said "Fighting like this has never happened here before". "This is sickening, behaviour like this will make parents not want to bring their children along." Another incident came midway through the second half when Rangers' supporters who had infiltrated the Portman terracing threw a smoke bomb which went on to the field.

Nottingham Forest Away. Our usual group of around a dozen got up to Nottingham for opening time. We went in a pub near to the station. I must have been out to a club the night before and not got changed because I was wearing Farah trousers, a Pierre Cardin jumper and fake croc skin shoes (yes I was a cheapskate). Not exactly the right attire for football and I felt a bit of a dick to be honest. We settled in this pub and the duke box was on, Red Red Wine by UB40 was being played over and over and that has stuck in my mind. There were only a dozen of us and time was getting on, I began to get a bit jittery, we had a bit of history with Forest and I didn't feel good about us being in a small group. I said to the lads I would go back to the station and wait for the next train in from London and show the next lot that arrived the pub we were in to boost up our numbers. This was way before mobile phones, so we could not even ring anyone up to see where they were.

I went on my own to the station and as I went through the entrance about ten Forest lads came straight at me. They saw what I was wearing and shouted at me "Oi you flash Cockney twat". As I said before I did not have much fear but this was a bit too much so I ended up running backwards and nearly got hit by a passing motor outside the station. As I backed off sharpishly and neared the pub again, another fella with a big perm and tash told the Forest lads to leave me alone. Fair enough they did and my bacon was saved for another mealtime in the future!

This chap with the Bryan Robson like hairdo seemed ok, he came back in the pub and introduced him to the rest. He sat with us for a pint, and yes UB40 was still banging out of the juke box. We asked this dude where the ground was from here, and what was the easiest way to get there.

He gave us directions and then he left and wished us all the best and may the best team win etc etc. No other of our lads had found this pub so off we went, the dirty dozen and followed the instructions of our friendly local.

We were all full of ourselves although a bit wary at the same time. We were walking alongside a river which must have been the Trent and approached the bridge which had a big pub on the end of it. A couple of punches were thrown at Forest fans who were walking by the side of us and just after that the doors to the pub opened and it seemed like a good fifty or sixty Forest came steaming out toward us. I didn't really want to run, but my mates were off and one had spotted a Forest lad with a small blade in his hand. So off we went over the Trent Bridge, one of our lads was caught at the back and received a mighty whack to his hooter. I think there is a pub called Hooters in Nottingham! We got to the other side of the bridge and there were a load of old bill there shepherding other fans toward the ground. They stopped us and the Forest mob done a U-turn and went back to their pub thankfully. My mate had just bought one of those Bennetton rugby shirts which was now red with his claret all down the front.

We went in the sets in the lower tier of their main stand and we saw the main lot who had mainly come on the coaches, typical we could have done with them being with us that day. The ironic thing was the geezer who had given us the directions spotted us from the top tier and shouted over "did you get here alright lads" and he was pissing himself along with a few other Forest chaps. We had been well and truly stitched up and set up for that little ambush back at the bridge, oh well that's the way it went.

Nottingham Forest Home 1. Around 1983/84, we were all meeting up a lot in the General Smuts pub right opposite White City pool. We had a good turnout which was the norm for those days. Everyone was buzzing for this as Forest was well up for it and always turned out in numbers. It was getting near kick-off time when one of our lads came steaming in through the door and announced that Forest had a good hundred and were rapidly marching down Blomfontein Road toward the Smuts. Everyone was out the door like rats up a drainpipe and we met Forest head on. The biggest memory that sticks out was the amount of diamond cut Pringles on show on both sides. Fair play to Forest they stood although they were slightly backed off and it was pure one on one punch-ups. This went on for a few minutes before the local constabulary arrived en masse. This was always a cue for everyone to keep walking as though nothing had happened, or straight back into the pub!

Nottingham Forest Home 2. This was a midweek night game in the League Cup I think. It wasn't a massive crowd and the weather was horrendous. It was freezing and had been snowing. Just before the kick-off the floodlights failed and the ground was left in total darkness. Myself and our usual crowd of about fifteen to twenty were sat in the corner of Ellerslie Road by the away end. As soon as the lights went out a mob of Forest appeared from nowhere and just steamed right into us. Fights were breaking out and bodies were tumbling over the seats. My mate who had his nose busted at Forest away took a bit of a slap again and had his brand new leather coat he bought that day ripped. He was one of the unluckiest fellas at football and by now must have hated the Nottingham lot with a passion!

I can't remember if the match was abandoned or not, but outside the ground was carnage, it was kicking off everywhere you looked. A minibus was spotted up by Wormholt Road and every window was put through as it sped off followed by a baying mob of R's lads. It was snowing again so that must have been one cold journey home for those boys.

Spurs Home. 1983/4 I think, all I remember about this game was after the match about thirty of us followed Gregor like the pied piper. We went down Loftus Road and then turned right along Uxbridge Road. Us youngsters were at the back and well buzzing for it. There are loads of side roads leading off and down one of them a large mob of Spurs were spotted heading down toward us. We took a charge toward them and to be honest I reckon Spurs thought there were a lot more of us as we were spread out across the road. No word of a lie they turned and ran back down towards the alley that led back toward the ground! It was around this era that there was a huge off on the green when a Spurs face got stabbed. I was not at that one but heard all about it. I am not saying in any way that QPR are in the same league as Spurs but we sure did ok in those days against them.

Leicester Home. This was an FA Cup match and a load of us all met up in what was then called the Bush Hotel on the corner of Goldhawk Road and Shepherds Bush Green. Not everyone had turned up yet as it was around lunchtime. Leicester must have got off at the station at the green and came marching along the Uxbridge Road. One of our lot saw them and guess who was out the door first, yes Gregor and a few us followed in anticipation. We ran toward them only to realize that not many had joined us, there was a brief stand-off and we headed back to the pub. Leicester must have been wrapped up further up the road. Nothing else happened until we entered the South Africa Road stand before the game. There was a good mob of Leicester in there and as usual they were escorted out before any real trouble started. After the game there was a massive head-on toe to toe on the Green. Old Bill vans even drove onto the green to break things up and nick a few people form either side. A great turn out from Leicester that day and respect for them arriving so early.

Man United (cockney reds) Home. This was a Friday night game which I think was one of the first live games on TV on a Friday around 1984 or 85.

United have always had a good following wherever they went and once again they bought good numbers. The attendances around those years had dropped due to all the violence at matches and this game was not a sell out if I remember correctly. For this match a lot of the older lot including the C-Mob went in the Ellerslie Road seats. United had a good firm of lads from all over London called the Cockney Reds and they had two very well known black geezers who I won't name. They both made their presence know that evening!

Toward the end of the game there was a small row up in the Upper Loft seats which included one of the fellas I just mentioned. At the final whistle around thirty of forty Cockney Reds must have sneaked in when the gates had opened and stood up the back of our seats in the Ellerslie. Obviously there was the usual surge toward them and they left and made their way down Loftus Road onto the Uxbridge Road toward the green. There were small running battles between each other all the way back to the station on the green.

Southampton Away. I went with the boys from Feltham in one of the lads motors. We lost the game as usual and the usual mob I knocked about was there. Everyone had the hump that we lost and the talk was everyone was going to march into town and kick off with Southampton, if we could find them.

There were only about twenty five of us who got it together and go into the town centre. There were a couple of young lads with us and they were sent ahead on a mission to see if there was a firm of Southampton about. We all waited, buzzing for it by a big roundabout not too far from the rail station. All of a sudden the boys came running back; "There's fucking loads of em" shouted one of our scouts and well out of breath.

About ten seconds behind them came a charge of about sixty of Southampton's finest. What struck me first was that their lad at front was shouting and had a scouse accent. Southampton is one of the biggest docks in the UK, and a lot of dockers came from Liverpool. We were outnumbered by more than two to one; this didn't usually bother me, but one of our lot made a decision; "Let's get back up on top of that railway bridge and hold them off there". That seemed a good idea; we all retreated and stood firm at the top of the small narrow footbridge over the railway tracks.

Southampton kept going past and over toward the station, we decided to go back through the station from the other side of the tracks and out onto the entrance.

We all stood in the forecourt of the station, and bottles started flying back and forth and smashing on the ground everywhere. There was one lone copper in the middle of us all trying to quell the baying mobs. He had no chance, my mate went to kick an oncoming Saint and he slipped over straight on his arse, I tried to shield him from the further onslaught. Then in a flash a Chinese lad came flying through the air Kung Fu style straight for my head, he even looked like Bruce Lee. I put my arm up and he connected with force. A few more punches were traded between the two groups and then the sound of sirens and the screeching of the tyres of several police vans.

Everyone dispersed quickly, and for once I went with them instead of carrying it on and getting nicked. We all made it back to the platform, everyone was hyper but still trying to look innocent at the same time. Thankfully no one was arrested. All the talk was of how well we had done to stand our ground with all the odds against us.

A train pulled in but it wasn't ours, a mob of around thirty blokes got off; "Here we go again" someone commented. The usual "Who are you lot?" came from their boy at the front. It turned out they were Bristol Rovers coming back from Portsmouth or somewhere. We told them we had just had it with Southampton and they were keen to team up with us and go back into town for some more. Everyone had had enough and wanted to get on the next train back to London. But we paid our respect to the Rovers lads and made our way back to the smoke and our nights out. I ended up going back to my local pub in Teddington. I was in agony all night and eventually went to the hospital where I found out my arm was broken.

Luton. We have always had a fierce rivalry with the boys from Bedfordshire and they have always been well up for it both home and away. One of the first ever bits of violence captured on CCTV was the St Pancras "affray" which I was not at. This was a revenge attack by our lot following slashings and beatings dished out to loads of our lads at one evening match at Luton. I am not sure if this was during the away fans ban at Luton or just a case of random attacks which were nasty. My mate Kev was one who received a bad one and another fella from Staines who has nasty scars down his boat race thanks to Stanley blades.

Luton was one of those games that would 100% go off whether it be on a large or smaller scale. My own personal experiences against this lot were firstly at theirs and I am not sure of the exact year but around 84. Luton would always be waiting as we made our way out of the side streets and onto the big main road. As we all got to the main road Luton made a charge at us expecting us to run, but we stood firm and it was toe to toe for a good couple of minutes before it all got broken up.

My next experience was in our ground up in the South Africa Road seats. About ten of us were in the block right next to the Loft, and all lads that went home and away together. A couple of the lads I have not seen for a many a year. Anyway, Luton scored and about ten of them jumped up to celebrate. A few warnings were dished out for them to fuck off as they were taking a liberty in our seats. They did settle down a bit but did not move away. Half time came and went and they were still there.

I can't remember the score in the end but at the final whistle we just steamed into them. A few lads went tumbling down the rows of seats on top of each other. Fair play they tried to hold their own. In those days there was no CCTV in the ground and for some reason that day there was a serious lack of stewards or old bill about. This went on for what seemed like a good five minutes which is a long time. Then we followed them out and let them go as the old bill had started to arrive.

The next one was at home again, this time I was with the main lot including the C-Mob in the Ellerslie Road. There was a good 80 – 100 of us in the seats together. Back then Luton had three brothers all in the squad I won't mention their name. At the final whistle a large mob of MIGS showed up at the back of the stand just like the cockney reds had done at that night match. It was the MIGS were goading us, fair play they were well dressed that day I remember loads of Armani jumpers on display especially the ones with stripes, I loved them with the golden Armani eagle on the sleeve. We were not having any of their piss taking and basically as they got outside we ran them down Ellerslie Road and all the way down toward Uxbridge Road. A few of them tried to make little stands but didn't fare well.

Over the years our battles with Luton have probably been about even stevens. The name MIGS was “Men In Gear”, and I personally think that was the most genius name for a football firm ever! Respect to Luton for that one.

Another lad remembers the SIMOD Cup final in 1988? “A bunch of us went to Wembley to get Luton, they were playing Reading. I got nicked walking up Wembley way , they found a kitchen knife on me. I don’t know how it ended up but it was in retaliation to the Rangers guy getting his face slashed in Luton.

Everton. Andy Nicholls the Everton lad wrote his book “Scally” and gave credit to QPR for one particular game against them. I am not sure if the following account is about the same game but it is taken from facebook;

PM Everton; We had a mad one in December 1983, the day IRA bombed Harrods. We never took that many to be honest, but about thirty of us were still walking around about an hour after the game. Eventually we found what we were looking for and more on Wood Lane I think it was. Bottles, CS gas, the Met old bill splitting our thrity up to send us opposite ways and hoping for us to get battered. We did well, both groups but could have been bad.

JM Everton: Goodison Park 1985 when we had already won the league. The last home game at Goodison v QPR, a great day and credit to the QPR fans that day too.

Arsenal (Latimer Road, Pig and Whistle). This was a huge battle that started from the Pig and Whistle pub. Arsenal known as the Herd in those days got off at Latimer Road tube station. There are many differing accounts of this one, and Arsenal like to say that it was mostly "locals" and not QPR. A little bit of denial there I would say. Here is what a good gooner mate of mine has to say about it;

On an old school website at Arsenal there's 750 lads on there. One of the boys asked about this off a couple of months ago. Most of our lot said they were pretty surprised at your turnout in fact you came out on top.(you get the usual we've never lost brigade) but all the good lads said they were really impressed with you lot. I heard that it all stemmed from a row between one of our lot, Donald a black lad from North London and had been threatened at Notting Hill carnival by some lads from the Grove (not football related). I think it spiralled from there? That makes a bit of sense because my mate Mark from the Grove was at the Pig and Whistle that day and he's not interested in football at all. He just went for a row (he's also a friend of Del's). I do know that the next pre season we were playing at Portsmouth and a coach load of ours left North London and got the driver to go via Ladbroke Grove and got off and walked into a few pubs. I can't really see why? It would have been full of shoppers and locals having a pint on a Saturday afternoon? To be fair that only proves you got the better of it on that day otherwise why bother going back six months later?

Liverpool Away 1985/86. Milk Cup semi-final. This account is written by Woody; It had been a great run in the Milk Cup (League Cup in old money) for me, that season, as I had only missed the second round away leg at Hull City. It is up there with the 1982 FA Cup run, where I only missed the Middlesbrough replay. Like for many R's fans, a refreshing change from the all too many seasons since of attending all the games in a cup run of one match. Cup Fever all too often being no more than a 24hr bug!

This cup run had already gifted two great away days. There was Watford, a ground we often struggled at in the 80's, where as usual we ran the gauntlet of allotments behind the away end in the pitch black and being herded onto a non-stop Euston train by the old bill, even though I only needed to go a couple of stops to Harrow to change for Ruislip. I ended up getting home just before the milkman, from a game just a few miles down the road. If that wasn't great enough, then there was Stamford Bridge a couple of months later and that Robinson goal from the half way line with the Rangers fans behind the goal almost sucking it over the muddy line.

I've been lucky enough to do 58 different away grounds following QPR. That said QPR are the club that just keep on giving for any fan trying to join the 92 club, by duly obliging and playing in three of the top four divisions in a relatively short period of time. But the stand out away day ever for me in this and all my seasons following QPR, is that Anfield trip.

I was nineteen at the time and at a stage in my life when I was playing Saturday football and suffering from Post Office's insistence on its employees providing a service six days a week, both of which was limiting my appearances down the Bush. But the Milk Cup was midweek games, and opened doors for me. In my school days, there were a handful of us that followed Rangers, one of whom was my mate Jez. I fondly remember our first steps into away days on the supporter's club specials in the early 80's. Jez had an older brother, Pete, and we often found ourselves making the numbers up in a compartment with Pete's mates, a pack of cards and crates of Long Life. I remember two of Pete's mates and seem to recall one called George who putting it politely was a bit dentally challenged and another Pete who had an amazing Dennis the Menace tattoo on his upper arm. These three lads took me and Jez under their wings, when we were new to the away day experience. And I am forever grateful for their guidance, their experience, the laughs we had and their help in such matters giving me some great memories and it is no exaggeration either to say giving me the nouse of how to look after yourself when travelling to pastures new.

There had been many trips on run down trains, squashed in the back of a Capri or worse, sitting on the floor in the back of a BT van trying to avoid the tools falling off their hooks. This Anfield journey began for me one night down The Black Bull in South Ruislip, the pub in the Inbetweeners sketch where the lads not only are in the wrong pub but they can't get served without ID, which wasn't a problem in our day. Jez says his brother could get us tickets on a private coach. I bit his hand off, well it was a semi-final and we deserved a bit of luxury. I forgot what it cost, but it couldn't have been too much, as I gave Jez my dosh there and then. We just had the little matter of the first leg to get over first. A 1-0 first leg win left the second leg nicely poised, and although I would have felt more comfortable had Fenwick's second "goal" not got chalked off for handball, we were very much still in it. The coach ticket decision proved to be a great one.

With the day off work sorted, myself and Jez made the short trip early in the morning from South Ruislip to Hammersmith, to board a Coach arranged by patrons of the Golden Gloves. My first ever taste of away day comfort. The seats that weren't slashed, glass in the windows, music coming out of speakers, heat coming out of the heaters, light bulbs that worked and it even had a TV at the front, not that we saw much sitting where we were near the back. A new law had been rushed through the year before, banning the carriage of alcohol on football coaches. We were not sure and had a small stash with us, enough to get us merry but not too much that it would have been painful to the pocket to have it confiscated on boarding the coach. But we needn't have worried as needless to say we weren't alone. Keeping the curtains closed was all that was asked of us.

The trip up was pure luxury to me, sitting in comfort reading the sports pages of all the national papers that seemed to be circulating around the coach. Seem to recall taking ages to get out of London, but once on the M1, the miles started ticking over nicely. If I was being picky, maybe the state of the on board loo even at this early point in the day, was starting to bother me. At that time I had a bowel capable of taking a good thrashing, but once the seal got broken I knew I would be up and down like a whores drawers. Within the first hour the single loo had already warmly welcomed forty plus cooked breakfasts, most of which appeared to include an extra side of black pudding. Although appearing to cope with the deluge it was the lack of air circulation that got up my nose, literally. But still ten times better than a loo on a football special

I may be wrong, but I don't recall us stopping until Anfield. Maybe the driver was keen to avoid a pub stop, and the inevitable well oiled passengers for the rest of the trip. Maybe the plan was to get us there as quickly as possible, to avoid any inquisitive panda cars passing by and pulling us over on the M6 and M62. Maybe he just fancied a plate of scouse for his lunch. I just remember we got to Anfield very early for an evening game, not that I was complaining

My first away day to Liverpool would have been five or six seasons before. I can never remember if it was Everton or Liverpool and doesn't really matter. What I do remember was it was the first time I'd been away and felt there was a real possibility this could go tits up. I wasn't worried about our fans, the train was full and we were amongst decent lads, likely to be out numbered but savvy and loyal. No sooner had we got off the train at the Sandhills station I think, we were herded into a car park to await the buses laid on to take us to the ground. Coppers on horseback saw the need to drum a tune on heads with their vintage three foot long wooden truncheons. No rhyme or reason, anyone over 5ft 10 that was too slow to duck. That was bad enough, but what got me was when we finally got on a bus it was driven through boarded up streets and across vast wastelands. Everywhere there were pockets of scousers peering out of smashed up houses, popping up on mounds of rubble in desolate plots that probably housed factories once. It reminded me of the John Wayne films my mum used to watch where John Wayne was taking a small troop of the Cavalry across bandit country with hordes of Red

Indians trailing them and popping up in little groups behind boulders and outcrops of cactus. It dawned on me, if the old bill didn't lay on the return buses after the game, I really didn't fancy the walk back to the train station. John Wayne may have made it back just with an arrow in his hat, but the Red Indians in the films didn't carry Stanley knives and Big John wasn't wearing decent clobber that was worth a few bob in some back street scouse pub or market. Thankfully for this trip, the coach took us straight to the Arkle pub, just a short walk from the away end. There were no bookies in sight where we pulled up, so Mr William Hill would have to wait another day for my gift of yet another fiver. My heart would have had us down for a win, but my head was worried if 1-0 would be enough against a team that was chasing a treble and made up of experienced internationals. So we got off the coach and into the pub. A handful of QPR fans were already in there, the long bar made it easy to get rounds in. This was our home for the next three or four hours. Not long after we arrived there was a skirmish outside, a group of scousers trying their luck on a small group of R's fans making their way to the pub and didn't expect to see a couple of coach loads in there already and were soon sent packing. I can remember a few ashtrays and bottles finding their way into pockets, many were expecting more trouble coming our way after that. The beer flowed, the crowd swelled as trains, coaches, mini buses of QPR fans arrived. Over the next couple of hours the pub became packed, many faces I recognized of blokes I didn't really know, slaps on the back glasses raised, singing, hugging. The pub had beams overhead, and I don't know how, but I remember a lad climbing up there which raised the singing level another notch. I don't remember him getting down, he was up there for ages much to the wasted efforts of the dissatisfied bar staff. The time came to leave for the ground, and pretty much as one we all made the short walk to the turnstiles, via a burger van of course, blue and white was everywhere. This was it, entering the cauldron of Anfield, with the mecca of the Wembley towers just a game away.

We were packed into one half of the Anfield Road stand. What struck me that night was the atmosphere we created. The singing never stopped, and I mean never stopped. One song led into another. Yeah the list of songs wasn't probably long enough for a twenty minute set, so there were a lot of repeats but I do know the answer was "yes" you bet Chelsea could hear us on the box. Not only did it not stop, but it was the whole end standing together and singing. I honestly couldn't hear anything coming from the Kop end, nor from scousers in the stands next to us. The game was a real cup tie with tackles flying in, both teams going for it which for me is in stark contrast to what gets served up and down the county now with football in comparison becoming very sterile. Sadly the atmosphere at football in general is something that has almost been killed off in the game now.

On the night most of the action was in front of the Kop, up the other end to us. As the game progressed a light mist, the sort of mist that you only get at winter evening games, come down on to the pitch. Not sure if it was mist rolling in off the Mersey or the smoke coming from thousands of nervous fans puffing frantically on fags that was turning the mist into a light smog. But both the distance and the mist were factors (perhaps along with the booze), which made us oblivious of the poor decision in the first half to award a penalty to Liverpool, the handball was way outside the box. Then there were no mobile phones to check, no large screen to watch so all that was left to do back then was join together in questioning the ref's parentage. During the second half when Liverpool went 2-1 up on the night 2-2 on aggregate, I soon realized I wasn't 100% sure what the rules actually were. Did away goals count double at 90mins, or was it extra time first? Neither was Jez or those around us, and different answers were only adding to my doubt. If it stayed 2-1 were we through, who knew, we just kept singing and got behind the lads.

Any concerns over the away goal rule were soon resolved when Fereday turned Hanson inside out and whipped in a cross for Robinson. Your natural reaction makes you get poised to celebrate as the ball gets anywhere near the goal, but the distance and mist made it difficult to see if Robinson was anywhere near the cross, let alone to get on the end of it. It went quiet around me as the Rangers faithful held their breath. Then time seemed to stand still, it was like all the players stopped moving and the floodlights got turned off as we couldn't see the ball moving. The only way I knew it was in was when Robinson got up off the ground and wheeled away celebrating, Jesus Christ he isn't celebrating a corner is he, it went in and the whole end erupted. What a feeling. I was hoarse long before then, but kept going even though my throat felt like it was full of gravel. I don't recall Liverpool having many chances in the second half and with an electric atmosphere around me oddly the minutes to the final whistle flew by for me. I know others will have had different thoughts about the final minutes, but I felt QPR were comfortable and invincible, they really put a great performance on in that second half. I don't know if we were locked in after the whistle or not, but I do know we were in there for ages, singing, jumping around and the players came over to us. We were on cloud nine and so where the players, the pride of West London was etched on all our faces. It always amazes me how stadiums seem to empty so quickly after the final whistle, except the one I'm in. Even now, how is it the stewards in Y Block manage to ensure it takes nearly fifteen minutes for me to get from my seat to the top of the exit stairs? Losing a semi-final you were expecting to win however only accelerated the scousers exit, the stadium was empty apart from our corner of W12. It seemed the decision to leave was made together and the crowd filed out together. It must have been thirty minutes or more after the final whistle. Outside the ground and making our way back to the coach there were a couple of skirmishes, scousers hanging back to throw a punch or kick before fading into the darkness. I shared a thought for any poor souls that had to make their way back to Sandhills station and I hoped for their sake the buses hung around for them.

Our coach journey home was a noisy affair, there was a

whip round as there were some cans being passed around. In truth I had had my full for the day and wasn't too disappointed there were no crates to get through. That said, my throat was burning and any liquid alcoholic or not, was appreciated. I remember the lads at the front were trying to get the driver to stop at a pub in Liverpool to get a few in before closing time. That didn't happen, as you can imagine the driver wanted to get us home as soon as he could. Whilst on the M6 and well past last orders, there was a lad at the front saying he had a mate who was a QPR fan and ran a pub in Stoke who would do afters for us. Needless to say it too didn't happen. God knows what time we got back to Hammersmith. Thanks to Jez though, we had already blagged a lift back to South Ruislip. It was only in that Capri that we both nodded off, good job I booked two days off work, I needed it.

I have been very lucky to have been at most of the games that are often talked about as the "I was there" games; WBA semi-final, 1982 Final and Replay, Sheff Wed promotion, Newcastle 5-5, Chelsea 6-0, Stamford Bridge 1-0, Oldham play off semi second leg and the Derby Play off final. But this game is my all-time favourite, and for me will never be bettered even if we were to beat Barcelona in a

Champions League Final with ten men.

Jez moved up north a few seasons later, but every season we still arrange a meet up at an away game half way for us both. He's the only mate from school I have kept in touch with and I will never forget him for sorting out those coach tickets, my best ever game, cheers Jez.

That is a great account of a typical away day from Woody there and I was also present at the game. I went up on a coach from the Goldhawk pub

And unfortunately I got nicked outside the Arkle pub before the match when it kicked off with the scousers. I was taken to Walton police station and luckily they let me out in time for me to enter the ground as we equalized.

I had to go back to court in Liverpool and had a right touch, a small fine which wasn't too bad.

Leeds Away. FA Cup 1987, Everyone was well fired up for this. Elland Road was not a place to visit for the feint-hearted. I was well chuffed to get a seat on the C-Mob coach that if I remember rightly left from the Princess Vic pub down the Bush.

All the main faces were on the coach this day and the fifty or so on board would have taken some shifting by anyone in the country with equal numbers. Anyone will tell you if they are honest enough that QPR's top fifty can match anyone.

The cans were being downed fast and everyone was in very high spirits. As we approached Leeds the coach was moving slowly through traffic, there were loads of locals looking at us and they knew who we were. A lot of our fellas wanted to get off the coach so we could make our own way in but the coach driver was having none of it. Finally we arrived in a big car park just by the ground. There was a big welcoming committee of old bill. As we stepped off the coach they were being heavy handed and kept us contained as they could see the possibility of a big off with the hoards of Leeds baying to have a go at us.

A horse stepped on one of our lad's foot, JJ was one of the best and has sadly since passed... RIP JJ. He went ballistic and was hopping around as the horses hoof must have dug right into him. Everyone thought that JJ was going to be nicked and luckily he was allowed to join us for our escort into the ground. There was loads of animosity from the home fans and there seemed to be thousands of angry

Yorkshire men baying for cockney blood.

We had a large section of seats in what I think was called the Lowfields stand and a small bit of terrace in the lower tier. We packed the allocation which was a good turnout from us especially at Leeds. Leeds also packed their whole ground a massive attendance for 1987 when crowds were down all over the country probably due to the violence of the times.

To our left outside the ground there was a big grassy hill and this was also packed with Leeds who didn't manage to get a ticket. A big percentage were all game geezers and on this day I have never seen so many nutters all in one ground, even more than the Old Den when I went there in 1988.

Our seats were only separated from the home fans by a line of stewards and old bill and throughout the game it looked like it was seriously going to kick off. There was a bit of a skirmish at half time down by the concourse area.

Leeds beat us 2-1 which was a bit of a shock as we were in the first division and Leeds in the second. At the full time whistle it seemed as though the whole ground came toward us and bless all the normal fans in the terrace below us were pretty much run out of the ground. For us in the seats it was a bit different, we had nowhere to go so we had to stand our ground and hold it all together. It really was a case of Custer's last stand and fair play we did as good as we could.

The old bill outside the ground had to hold back the hoardes of Leeds and there were literally thousands of them. We made it back to our coach and at the first service station we stopped at a few Leeds on their way home got a bit of a slap just out of spite.

Sometimes especially back in those days trouble would escalate on different occasions away from the match day itself.

QPR had a bit of history with various fights in the Lyceum night club with Arsenal.

One incident that I was present at occurred on my pal's eighteenth birthday celebration. A load of us decided to go on the piss in Chertsey in Surrey. At the time there was the Galleon pub, the Cricketers over the road and a nightclub known simply as “The Lock”.

The Galleon would often get groups of both lads and girls on a good night out from other areas all around West and South West London.

We had a tight little group of QPR lads as I have mentioned previously from Bush, Edgware Road, Feltham, Teddington and even from Chertsey itself.

This was at the height of the “Casual” scene, the clothing was colourful and a lot of gold jewellery would be worn such as sovereign rings and belcher chains. Some lads even wore heavy gold rope chains round their next, not quite Mr T from the A Team but not far off!

Anyway, when our mate turned eighteen, that weekend QPR were playing at Birmingham away. I had never been to Birmingham myself and was really looking forward to that one. Birmingham were notorious with their firm the “Zulus”. Not many teams could go up there and return home without any casualities.

If I remember rightly it was also the FA Cup semi-final weekend and a big London team was travelling up to Villa Park that same Saturday. So to say it was going to be eventful was an understatement!

Everyone was up for having a great evening, there was about fifteen of us all told and we started off in the Galleon. The music of the time was Jazz Funk and soul, who remembers “I found Lovin” by Steve Walsh who tragically died too young. This was a banger of a tune and so was “Last night a DJ saved my life” great times!

I used to get hammered all the time, I was an alky which I have now addressed. I was always a bit angry and probably didn’t enjoy the craic like most of the other lads. Basically I was always on alert to just kick off for any excuse.

I was going to stay at my mate’s house that evening with another couple of the boys and we were going to head up to Euston in the morning for a good old fry up in one of the cafes around there.

A good little firm of us was going to Brum, it was going to be good.

Back in the Galleon, the more pints that were being necked, the louder we got. And then we started singing QPR songs, as you do. What we didn’t realize was that there was a local mob of Chelsea around the other side of the boozer. They were getting the hump, we were on their patch and saw it as a bit of a piss-take.

We found out later they were from Addlestone, which is not far from Chertsey and they had a good few game chaps who were Chelsea.

As we left the pub we started to walk over the Chertsey Bridge, still singing as we went.

The Addlestone firm came charging out behind us with an announcement of "We're Chelsea, let's have it" you all know the one!

Bang! It all went off and we certainly got the better of them one of their lot got taken to hospital. The old bill were on the scene very lively indeed.

I had been nicked so many times back in those days, I had no sense to turn it in and walk away. So I was still at it calling at the Chelsea boys as they were on the retreat. I got collared by a copper from behind who had my arms bent up my back and about to put me in cuffs.

My first reaction was to headbutt the officer with the back of my head. Apparently he bit through his tongue. I got a severe kicking back at the nick and I did not calm down until I eventually went down on the floor. The fuckers didn't even leave me a blue mattress I had to wake up stiff as a board on the bare floor.

My mate had been nicked but let out without charge and made it to meet up with the others and go the Brum.

I was living with another good pal of mine and his family at the time and thankfully they came and collected me around midday the next day.

For that little adventure I had to go back to Chertsey Magistrates court and received a three month detention centre sentence.

Just another occupational hazard, or just plain stupidity and drunknenness? I know the answer now.

Most books like this are usually from the fan's perspective, the following story is how QPR's chief steward remembers the events at our FA Cup game with West Ham in 1988.

"We played West Ham a week after we had previously played them, the counter foil tabs were not removed in that first game so the supporters presented them again at the turnstiles and were let in.

It became obvious something was wrong when the school end became crowded and was starting to overspill.

The police decided to relieve the congestion by getting the fans on the pitch behind the police horses to move them into the Loft where there was some space.

I must have been sorting out a problem with turnstiles or the box office, when I got back on the pitch the police and West Ham fans were on the halfway line.

I ran out to the centre circle with both arms outstretched to halt them.

The officer in charge told me what he was going to do I said you can't do that it would cause a riot. What do you suggest he asked?

I said I would move the fans out of the east paddock as they were Rangers Fans and move them into the Loft through the side gate but it was better to take them out of the ground and bring them back in through the main Lower Loft entrance.

He gave me ten minutes to get this done, I think it took a

little longer but he could see I was achieving what I said I would do.

The West Ham Fans were put into the east paddock and the game kicked off I think about thirty minutes late.

The officer in charge at the end of the game thanked me.

This is how a good friend of Dave's remembers that day. "On one occasion we had an overspill of about two thousand fans due to forged tickets. (It turned out that they were not forged as Dave explained re the counterfoils) You were at your best that day. You grabbed a bull horn and persuaded eighteen hundred fans to move out of the East Paddock and moved them to the family stand which allowed the overspill of mainly West Ham fans to be accommodated. You really put a flea in the Polices ears that day. There were many more occasions when you deserved a medal for your leadership during that period. (There was also a time when Dave managed to calm down a mob of QPR from steaming into a load of Luton up in the South Africa Road seats. He had a way with the lads and was well respected. Not like the Gestapo stewards of today.)

Thanks to Dave Webber for this contribution and respect

from myself for your efforts back in the day when hooliganism was rife.

3 BATTLE OF BARNET

I am now going back well before my time and an infamous QPR match against Barnet in 1972/73. The tie went to a replay at Barnet and for some reason there was a whole load of trouble and was dubbed "the battle of Barnet!"

I have had a few accounts from the older fans of QPR and here are a few little versions of events. One question I asked was "Why?" it seemed a bit strange that there would have been such a turnout from both sets of fans for a club like Barnet.

"I think we had built such a bad reputation during those years, maybe this was a chance for them to get at us, at a small ground where they didn't think there would be many old bill and we would probably run amok.

We all met up before the game in a local pub. When we left there were around a hundred of us. We quietly marched on towards the ground it was like a military operation. We had heard that all the London clubs were going to join forces, and would be waiting for us in their end. E entered the ground at the opposite end to theirs. Then we went, almost single file towards the war zone. Upon arriving at their end people in there started moving away from us. In those days trouble brewing was always obvious. When there were enough of us it started. They soon knew who we were with the loud and constant "Rangers boys are here" chanting. Before the game started we were attacked from the left side. Police formed a line between us and an increasing growing group of rivulet soldiers. This line was often broke and some of the police retreated injured by flying objects. I don't think many in that area saw much of the game as the skirmishes went on throughout the game. Both sides had injuries, but we held our ground against other mobs, in great numbers, mostly Arsenal and Chelsea. I am certain the reputation of The Loft as a force to be reckoned with was enhanced as a mob to beware of after this game.

Other accounts from QPR fans;

I was in the stand to the left of the away end, it was very nasty. The St. Johns ambulance were leading fans with bleeding heads down the touchline to the far corner of the ground all game.

This was a battle from the moment we arrived to the moment we left, it was like the whole of London against The R's! Rocks were bouncing off the roof from one side to the other and vice versa, I've never seen so much violence during one match within a ground!

It was unbelievable, we entered the ground at one end and stood at the far end of the ground. There was continuous aggro throughout and it didn't stop there, outside was even worse, serious running battles!

I had to watch for flying bricks from outside the ground, and had only just started dipping my toe into that side of the game. So it was quite an eye opener when after one surge I found myself right at the front and punches were flying everywhere.

I've never been so scared at a football match, bricks were flying everywhere they knocked a wall down and just started throwing them. They even climbed on the terrace roof to throw them down at fans. After the game it was just running battles all over. There were mobs from every club in London who just steamed in for the plentiful cheap tickets and a chance of a quick smash and grab row!

Later in the 1970's the C-Mob was born. As I have said earlier, from the late 1970's and early 1980's most teams up and down the country had a "firm". Some were much bigger in numbers and more well known.

I have mentioned the Leeds Service Crew, one of the most notorious mobs was West Ham's ICF and they even had a younger lot known as the Under-Fives which is a genius name.

QPR's boys decided to call themselves the C-mob and were formed in 1979. About forty or fifty or so go good mates went up in a coach to Preston away. This is where the name "C" Mob came about. C being "coach" which is how these lads travelled about. And even if it was a midweek game at some rotten old Northern town they would still go in a mini-bus.

No one can ever say that the C-Mob were not game as fuck,

they could hold their own against anyone with even numbers and that is a fact.

What I like about C-mob is that they have never felt the need to write any books or big themselves up to any one. They have kept everything low key, and respect for that.

I am not sure if they will have the hump with me for writing this book, but for me it is something I wanted to do as I have a passion for all things QPR.

In the 1980's everyone was trying to take each other's ends. The C-mob tried at various grounds to do that and have done successfully on numerous occasions. But admittedly have come unstuck loads and that is due to the fact there was probably never more than fifty of them.

A funny story that one of the old regulars told me was when they went in Bristol Rovers home end one Tuesday night game. They admit they got battered and a couple of lads had to go to and get stitched up at hospital. The old bill took them out of the Rovers end and escorted them round the pitch back to the away end.

As they passed the dug out, our manager Terry Venables saw what had happened and said to one of the chaps who had blood pouring out of the back of his head.... "Are you OK son!"

Around that era of the early mid 80s the C-Mob mainly drank in the Princess Victoria pub along the Uxbridge Road. A lot of the bigger firms would head there and had there hands full to be sure.

My pal says that the only time that the C-Mob didn't stand any chance of offering a good go was when they got run by the ICF all the way from near the ground back to the Princess Vic again. Chelsea usually took over our ground due to the amount they bought. That does not happen nowadays.

When I get the chance to go back to watch the R's home or away I still see a good few of the old C-Mob fellas and of course we are all getting older and wiser now and staying out of trouble.

4 GREGOR

Every football club up and down the country has a set of lads that stick together and even now will meet up every now and then. Football violence is a thing of the past and anyone with any sense would have called it a day long ago.

However the old stories from back in the day still make us laugh and reminisce of those crazy times. If you want to hear a story or two then Gregor is your man. I could listen to him all day and he has me in stitches with his amusing banter. I asked him if it's ok to put a few memories in this book and of course he agreed.

Gregor could write his own book, in fact he could write a series. Another top man from the old days is Annis from Cardiff and he has written a series of books based on the

Soul Crew. Both Gregor and Annis have a mutual respect for each other even though the rangers and Cardiff have had serious run-ins over the years.

They have both saved each other's bacon when it has come right on top. I will start Gregor's stories with the time that QPR were playing the Welsh mob one home night game. Around sixty Cardiff youth had spotted Gregor, it was pitch black down Blofonteim Road. Gregor was only with a couple of other lads and he was surrounded by an angry sixty baying for his blood. Annis stepped in and told the young-uns to leave him alone. Gregor had done the very same for Annis on another occasion.

Earlier I mentioned about the big row with Arsenal at Latimer Road and Gregor has a funny tale about that day. He says that Arsenal got off the tube train and came to the Pig and Whistle pub where a big mob of QPR had met up. Some of the gooners came to the door and Gregor greeted them with "Congratulations you've just met QPR!" This was a famous saying doing the rounds and started by West Ham's ICF. Anyway rangers steamed out the door with pool cues and bottles etc and managed to back Arsenal off to the flyover under the Westway motorway. It was kicking off and little battles all round. Old bill had got wind and one particular copper had been gunning for Gregor. The officer managed to get Gregor to the floor and pinned him to the ground with a big sheet of board that was lying around. The old bill excitedly announced to his colleagues "I've got him, I have been waiting for this for five years!" Gregor still laughs when he tells this even though he was nicked.

QPR have had some good ones with Middlesbrough mainly back in the 1980's. One game we were playing them at home and Gregor decided to head up to Kings Cross station hours before the game. He went with Chelsea's Fat Pat and another well known lad from the R's MS. Basically they went up there to see the Boro firm arrive and see what they were up against that day. Boro turned up with a massive mob and Gregor described them as all massive big lumps. Gregor was well known to many other teams around the country and one Boro lad spotted him and fronted him up in the station. "Where's your boys, you are that bloke from QPR?" the chap from Teeside asked. Gregor admits he had to think sharp and get out of his predicament, he mumbled back that he was "Brentford!" Somehow he got away with that one and says he has on quite a few occasions been lucky to escape a good hiding.

They now knew what they were up against and headed back to Shepherds Bush and carried on wandering around various pubs.

Gregor says that Boro must have got off at Barons Court near Hammersmith in order to not get spotted by the old bill. He says that two massive mobs of Boro must have converged at the petrol garage right on the corner of Shepherds Bush Green. There were at least 150 to 200 of them and very game looking geezers and the size of Popeye's arch enemy Brutus!

Gregror must have known that QPR's C-Mob were mainly in a pub up Goldhawk Road the Shepherd and Flock. Boro started to head the other way and Gregor shouted at them "You're going the wrong way!" He managed to rapidly get back in the pubs door well ahead of Boro. When he entered the Flock about fifty good QPR lads were sitting around having laughs and playing cards.

"They are here, Boro are on their way now" One of the chaps asked how many there was. Gregor replied "Only thirty or forty" which he knew was bullshit!

Rangers were straight out the door and launched straight

into the oncoming Boro firm. The C-Mob backed them off twice before they realized there was only smaller numbers of QPR. Then it started coming on top a bit for the rangers lot. QPR did well and Boro were taken by surprise.

The following season Gregor says that Boro came back again with an even bigger army and that again he was collared by a Boro lad the size of Giant Haystacks. The lad pointed to his Boro pin badge and told Gregor that when he catches him he will make him kiss the badge!

One thing about Gregor he is always honest and admits when QPR have been done or outnumbered and that personally has had to retreat or be battered. But no one can take away the fact that he always put his neck on the line for QPR.

Some other good games that Gregor mentions are a time when Aston Villa came to QPR maybe back in the 80's. There were about 250 Villa and were well away from the ground near the other side of the White City estate. They must have come from East Acton or gone the wrong way from White City station. QPR had good numbers too and Villa was shocked at the gameness of the rangers lot that day.

There was the big one with Everton when they were caught out down Wood Lane which was described in the book "Scally". Gregor says Everton came back the following season with huge numbers and did well. One Everton lad on facebook "PM" says "Everton Had a mad one in December 1983, the day IRA bombed Harrods. We never took that many to be honest, but about thirty of us was still walking around about a hour after the game. Eventually we found what we were looking for and more on Wood Lane I think it was. There were bottles and CS gas and the Met old bill split our thirty up to send us opposite ways, hoping for us to get battered. We did well, both groups but could have been really bad.

"JM" Everton, At Goodison Park in 1985 when we already won league. It was the last home game at Goodison v QPR and was a great day. Credit to the QPR fans that day too.

Another funny one that Gregor speaks about is a day when Fulham were home to Port Vale and QPR were also at home. QPR decided to go down to Fulham after the game, Gregor and a couple of others spotted about fifty Port Vale drinking in a pub down the Fulham Palace Road. The Vale spotted Gregor and they piled out of the boozer and gave chase for about fifty yards and then saw a good fifty of rangers' finest coming at them. Gregor says it was hilarious watching fifty big fat lumps all trying to leg it back through one doorway of the pub!

Another book written was Sheffield United's Blades Business Crew. In the book it describes how their mob took liberties at QPR one season, in the 1990's if I remember correctly. Gregor wants to set the record straight here as do a lot of other R's that I know. After that particular match a good mob of the Blades were run down South Africa Road and the honours were certainly more even than the book describes. Too many of these teams make out that they were never turned over or make things sound better for them selves than was really true. I personally am not taking anything away from Sheffield United but sometimes you have to admit what really happened.

It was maybe a season or so after that one that I went to Sheffield United and we only met up with about thirty or forty of us. We sat in some pub which was about a fifteen minute walk from the ground. Our old bill spotters were keeping a close eye on things and came in to the pub and told us there was a mob of over a hundred Blades waiting for us further down the road. They said they would give us an escort, and back in those days I was always well on the piss and lairy as fuck! I told our FIU friend to stick the escort as we were making our own way to the ground. Forty of us marched up to the ground, admittedly with a dozen or so old bill keeping close tabs on us from behind. We went straight to the ground without seeing one Sheffield fella. And that is the truth. And I am not saying we took the piss but just telling it as it was on that day.

Going back to the 1980's and Gregor, he wanted me to mention how he formed a group of lads which he called the "Ellerslie Enders". When he said that it rekindled my memory and I now do remember that.

Ellerslie Road stand is the one tier of seats along the side to the left of the home end. There used to be a kind of metal doorway which led into the away end. And at some games this was unmanned by stewards or old bill. Gregor's band of merry men would try and get through this gate and into whoever we were playing. One game that Gregor mentions was against Liverpool. He says a good twenty five "Ellerslie Enders" made it through and had a good battle with the scousers. There were a good few times like this and of course this all ended toward the end of the 80's.

The final memory from Gregor is another one that he laughs about and is hilarious. Gregor was a good pal of Chelsea's Fat Pat and when Pat sadly passed (RIP) he attended his funeral. Gregor says he was a bit wary of going to pay his respect because there would be reps from all other different teams present. And Gregor admits himself he was not the most popular geezer in the football world!

He says it was like a gangster's funeral, loads of proper people there. A minibus pulled up which happened to be Cardiff's main lads. One fella got out and noticed Gregor straight away, he came straight over. Gregor was unsure how this was going to pan out and the Welsh chap announced "Alrite Gregors the last time I saw you, you was chasing me with your toe right up me arse!" I [pissed myself when he told me that one and he said they all had a good grin over that at the funeral and there was no animosity.

Gregor (at the time of writing) has recently been accused of being a racist. He has been threatened and even had to move area. I can assure anyone that if there is anyone I have met that is not racist in any way, then that is Gregor. He has been a youth football coach for many years and helped many local black kids to get into the game. I have seen Gregor around the Bush on non match days having banter with everyone, no matter where they are from.

Gregor is one of those characters you could describe him as "Marmite!" Love him or loathe him, I personally think he is a diamond, we all have our faults but at the end of the day if you are reading this book then you must relate to him in some way.

Funnily enough there was another lad at QPR who was the same height and even had the same wedge haircut. Here is a funny story he remembers;

I do remember being chased down Uxbridge Road with a few lads by Gooners. They were all Dressers shouting out to me thinking I was Gregor. We were totally outnumbered, there was no way I was standing. They had loads that day not sure of the year. I often got mistaken for Gregor!

This book is mainly about the 1980's and the Casuals that we all became, maybe some of you didn't and were just into the football and being with the lads.

A respected lad who supports Oxford United was kind enough to find the time to tell this little story.

A massive thanks to KP;

"Kevin stop!" I turned around instantly not really recognizing the voice, to my shock at a second glance, it was a lad I played footy with on a Saturday. But only on rare occasions, and I certainly didn't know he was a copper, later to become our police intelligence officer PC "P". It was kicking off in Carfax, Oxford's city centre and I was just launching a raid into enemy territory. It is surprising how only moments earlier I wouldn't of given two fucks and would of gone through the old bill like a knife through butter. But it stopped me in my tracks he knew who I was no matter what it's not something you expect is it, especially back then. It was a decent little off and quite sporadic, and no victory was noticeable for either side. I am m only talking about when we arrived and not before, there was undercover old bill in attendance and lots of old bill was the only spoiler. The lot I was with came from the Ale House, I'm sure it was called that back then. It was formerly the Paradise and Culture Vulture, a decent pub and where the older Oxford used to go long before this particular game. I will never forget that around mid day, I was sitting at the back of the pub having a drink with a few lads waiting on the forthcoming activities when the door opened and in bowls the Aylesbury lot. I was in a bit of shock, as I knew they held allegiance with QPR but also had started to come to Oxford. And to be fair they were sound lads, bar one and always well dressed. They came in and came straight to me. "QPR are wanting it and are waiting for you and us." They were only relaying a message, but I stupidly felt betrayed and know a couple of mates felt the same. What side are you on I thought, leading to an eventual fall out between a few of them and a row too. Looking back now I was wrong to even think that, but at the time I was none the wiser. I was right in my own head I suppose. The fallout was finalized when myself and CK got it put on us at a night game at theirs, in the backstreets by one of them a year later. I was not with the lads mentioned though, let's be honest now, they was only bringing food to the table, which I soon digested. After the game a mob of us headed towards the train station as we knew they had been given an escort and was just out of sight from the watching old bill. We hid quietly down an alley and just by chance spotted crates of empty bottles. As the QPR mob walked past, we launched virtually every bottle, and in a split second we started to run. I am not sure why, but we did and it was just a reaction. I can't really explain, you could say we bottled it, excuse the pun but for me more of a case of getting away from the old bill. But fair play to them it didn't stop them coming at us and we all split up, some of us stood firm and little skirmishes carried on into the town centre, even in one of the main shops that was closing. I've always respected QPR, especially after being given a pass with CK when we decided to have a look in their seats and nearly came a cropper at half time down at the back. I was just about to lash out, and one of them said leave them even though most wanted to seriously waste us. So after a little chat I promised to head to the Bush after the game, which never materialized. The respect I have for Rangers has only grown over the years, especially after making friends on social media with quite a few QPR lads, and with me getting an invite to D's baby's head wetting. L came to meet me and sorted me out proper before introducing me to all the lads. Funnily enough I heard Mr Gregor was going to be there, so I decided to take a framed photo of the incident in the town centre thirty years earlier, which one of our lads had taken a picture of. It is a picture of the row I mentioned and it has me following Mr Gregor trying to say hello! I do remember a few more incidents with QPR, ones I was involved in, but one I sadly missed was at Wembley after the game.

Unfortunately I wasn't there so can't really comment. But I heard it was a little on top. General Jeff James, who is sadly no longer with us, always had a soft spot for QPR after he was involved in plenty of incidents and always rated them, as Oxford always did. Jeff was also a guest a few times at Rangers and was even there when they kicked off in a right good row with a Northern firm. Jeff told me how decent they were and said they were game as fuck. When our Jeff sadly passed away recently, the Rangers lads collected a large amount of money to put towards Jeff's funeral, they also brought beautiful floral tributes, to show their respect for someone, not only loved by Oxford but the whole country. I just can't say in words how much respect I have for QPR on and off the pavement. I will finish my bit here with one of our lads, who has many more stories than me involving QPR and what he said straight after the wake for Jeff. He was part of the mob that took over us older lads. They are the South Midland Hit Squad. This is what he said after the wake, I quote; "It was surreal seeing Gregor eating an ice-cream outside one of our boozers, something you could never have imagined back in the day....Respect.

Another top Oxford lad "T" recalls;

This is from "T", Oxford had a link with QPR through a small crew from Aylesbury who started to come to Oxford games when we were going up into the top Division in 2985. A couple were Oxford but most were QPR and the QPR lot came to our big home games. They were all a clued-up bunch; older and wiser than most of us; as 75% of Oxford were sixteen to eighteen back then.

Oxford played QPR five times in 1986:

1st Jan 86 (A) New Year's day trip to Loftus Road. No clashes but both had a lot out. We bumped into the Aylesbury QPR lot and it was a bit tense considering our main faces knew them well.

29th Mar 86 (H) QPR showed their class. We were dotted around our town centre (as you did back then) and they arrived off the train, lead from the front by MG and with the local knowledge of the Aylesbury firm, they steamed anything we had. We were not organised, stood around in small groups and got ran or smashed. Oxford got it together after the game and they came around looking again but nothing happened. It was too late; the damage had been done. It was a hard but valuable lesson.

20th Apr 86 Milk Cup Final at Wembley – Oxford's greatest day on the pitch and we faired better off but again QPR were just better that day and though it was more even than the game a few weeks beforehand; they had the better. Oxford took a huge firm but it was again disorganised and so we split up. Again we bumped into a few of the Aylesbury lot on Wembley Way and again it was a bit tense – that relationship had soured! After the game there were many clashes on the tubes, some we did ok in but one near Baker Street (where I was) we got blitzed. At Paddington we regrouped and were ready but they somehow mingled in and so when the roar went up; we were in disarray and half of ours got run down the platform and the rest were on the concourse puzzled. We had another go but the Met stopped that and we lost out on what could have been a great battle.

15th Nov 86 (A) Possibly the largest mob we'd taken away, on the early train – it was time to get organised. The Met were on us and so the day was spent trying to get away from them and so sadly nothing happened. QPR told us to go to Ladbroke Grove after and we tried but the Met were tight that day. But we felt the tide was turning with our numbers and being better organised. This would become effective for the last game we played that year.

27th Dec 86 (H) This time in town we met in two pubs and kept in contact so had eyes all over. We still didn't know how QPR got to a pub on the back street but they were a classy outfit and so no surprise there. We knew they were there and waited in groups and they came – they bounced up the main road and our two groups joined and we met head on (this was known ever since as the battle of Carfax). They seemed shocked but this was the first time we'd met them mob on mob – they came again, we went in again and whilst neither firm budged; we felt we had the upper hand considering the previous games. The filth moved in as some of theirs tried again and MG and RC got pulled. We were buzzing and went to the ground looking for it. We bumped into two Aylesbury who had taken a bit of a slap at Carfax and they said that this was QPR's top firm which was nice to hear.

After the game we went early to town to wait. Some of ours walked down in front of their escort as it was walked into town by our plod. Oxford had a hundred plus and waited behind some restaurants in a dark side road near the station; knowing they'd have to come past. The lads in front gave us five minutes notice and there happened to be crates full of empty Britvic bottles (the small ones) so we grabbed loads and went to the end of the road. They appeared, we roared and unloaded our arsenal of tiny bitter lemon bottles. Speaking to them in later years; they said the sky went black (even though it was black anyway at 6pm in December!) but the street lights were blocked out. In fairness to them, they ran through the barrage and the firms clashed but not for long as the filth were already there so easy for them to split us up. We both went our separate ways and that was when we knew we had matched them when at the start of the year it was men against boys.

A couple of weeks after the game on our lunch break; I saw MG dressed up so presumed he was in court for the battle of Carfax. We went to the College to round up a couple more and went to the station with five of us. He was there waiting for his train and we approached for a chat as he was alone – then RC came from behind and pushed one of our black lads and then we faced off but to be fair; we were unsure as knew of his rep and the blade rumours; so when a train guard said he was calling the ob; we took the chance to leave it. One of the most interesting lunch breaks I've ever had!!

We played twice in 87 – the away game was again non-eventful but we took a decent firm - the Met just seemed to have it sorted for us out-of-towners! At the home game at Oxford it was far easier for us. They didn't bring such a good firm and ours was growing in numbers, confidence and quality, so when we met before and after; both results were ours. Also after the game; the town blacks joined us, as they started to do in 87 as they realised it was such fun!! Some of ours went down for the home game.

We then didn't play until 95 and although there were minor clashes in the 90s; nothing compared to 86/87.

I last saw the full Aylesbury (QPR) firm in Nov 87 when they went to Bristol City in the FA Cup. They had a decent outfit that day but don't think City came out to play. "T".

This is what it is all about now, a mutual respect between like minded lads who are now all long retired from the football hooligan scene. There still are some idiots who try and belittle QPR but maybe that is sour grapes and something I will never lower myself to.

5 OTHER LAD'S ACCOUNTS

These are some selected memories of incidents from R's fans who have kindly contributed to this book;

Neil.

As an outsider to Rangers close knit group of lads from the Bush or Grove I found out very quickly in the Early/ Mid 80,s, after you looked older than a schoolboy you were fair game. In about 1984 myself and a couple of close mates decided after getting a slap at Hammersmith Station from older Chelsea lads we had to choose one of two paths. Finally walking into a ferocious scrap at the bottom of the escalators at Liverpool Street station with West Ham after a trip to Ipswich, I decided being part of it was the way forward. Looking back now without rose tinted specs,

London was then a very much more violent place than it is today. It even seemed quite normal for a punch up to happen at a Specials gig, a nightclub or even walking down Kings Road wearing the wrong clothes. Football was this magnified by ten!

In 1986 new friendships were formed and the Princess Victoria pub was the pre match local and there were so many characters. I took to big Ron, recognizable by his copy of the Daily Mirror hanging out of his back pocket. Ken a greengrocer from the Grove and especially JJ a larger than life Character from Hayes. It was a real shock to hear in February that JJ passed away on 08/02/2019 and he was given a tremendous send off with a Coach and Horses and Rangers anecdotes through the service. I forgot to mention Vic who sneaked me into the Hammersmith Odeon a few times when head of security and looked after the special away trains and apart from being Mr QPR one of the nicest men on the planet.

I'm sure this will be a common thread throughout by the book but "That" night game we had with Luton in 1987 was the most brutal and hate filled atmosphere I've ever witnessed . Fixtures against Luton were escalating over the years but that night was a war zone and witnessed some horrific sights. Myself and two other friends arrived into Luton Station about five O'clock and scouted the station for familiar faces but didn't see anyone so left the station and headed for a pub we had used before. Anyone who has been to Luton will know the sixties built rat run of stairs and linking underpasses are an ambush paradise. Turning right and into the second underpass a group of Luton spotted us and one chap pulled a very large knife out of his jacket and another of the group started swinging a sock full of pool balls around as we tried to get to the top of the stairs . Stuart my mate copped a nasty blow and needed stitching up. Luton had obviously set this up as we got to the end of the underpass thirty or forty Rangers were outnumbered but fighting back by a parade of shops. Needing to assess my mate's injury we went in a corner shop and immediately had to empty the fridge of cans of Fanta and Coke at Luton. I saw one of ours take what I though was a sly punch but soon realised as he held his scalp he had a large knife wound and needed immediate help. By the time the Police turned up it was done and we had to get my mate sorted so by that time we made our way to the ground. Once in the away pen at Kenilworth Road similar stories were coming out and a number of ours had been taken to hospital with serious wounds and anger and retribution along with the shock at what happened was just hitting home. I saw a fella I knew by face and sure he was a Feltham lad with serious lumps over his head looking like the Elephant Man and couldn't believe he didn't want attention. He had also met the sock full of pool balls earlier. Although this was pre mobile phone era, we tried to get news of my mate from the hospital and we missed Part Two after the game where apparently we had serious revenge and got some retribution. I am not ashamed to say that evening's events gave me a few sleepless nights in years to come.

In 1985 Oxford achieved promotion to the top flight for the first time and instantly we had a great away day and almost instant rivalry. I have a lot of respect for Oxford and they were far from shabby in the 80's. After two eventful trips to The Manor Ground including a mad 3-3 draw which drew the biggest firm I've witnessed out of town we managed to meet them at Wembley for the Milk Cup final. The less said about that the better! The team didn't turn up we lost 3-0. In house fighting erupted between Rangers factions around Wembley long before the third goal finished the game as a contest. We were at best pathetic and many Rangers left for the exit long before the final whistle full of frustration and anger. As we walked down Wembley way we met up with a few more old faces and decided a little trip to Paddington to give our new friends a nice send off. By the time we got to Wembley Park our numbers had snowballed to about sixty and thought this would be a nice meet and greet at Paddington and we waited by what was in the old station Taxi rank by the main platform. After about an hour enough of Oxfords finest had congregated on the main concourse and platform we thought now was a good a time as ever as nothing was suspected at all. The usual roar went up and we went straight into the first pocket of Oxford who made a hasty retreat and at first had no retaliation. It wasn't until a few of their main boys caught on to the skirmish and then realized we were outnumbered badly that they started holding their ground. After about two minutes of full on fighting the cavalry then arrived in the shape of the Met old bill and batons were drawn and dogs involved and many collars felt and the last thing I wanted was to be arrested as I got nicked against Liverpool in the semi final. I got a smack on my shoulder from a older copper and evaded him and looked at my other mates and five of us decided to get on the train and take our chances as it was full of Oxford but still evading the old bill was the higher priority. Luckily enough in all the confusion we slipped the attention from the police and the train started departing the station which diffused the situation on the platform but we had been spotted and punches were exchanged and we decided to run through all the carriages to the end and barricade the door shut. All I can say is thank god the old style doors had sturdy handles and the door opened inwards so we blocked it up with the fire extinguisher which were much bigger in the old days and talked about the great escape.

I knew the journey would take about twenty five minutes to Reading but it seemed like an eternity and we could hear the threats from the other side of the door about what was going to happen to us along with the bangs which didn't help. Everyone on that train wanted our blood, we chatted about pulling the emergency cord but that could go horribly wrong so plan B it was. One of us looked out of the window and it seemed that every window in every carriage heads were out giving us nice gestures, this was not going to be easy. For the youngsters once again luck was on our side and on the old slam door trains you could open and shut them when you wanted not just when the guard or driver released them. Plan B was to assess very quickly if there were fifteen or less and stand and give it a go and good luck. As we approached Reading one of my mates nearly left the train earlier than expected as he was making sure the door did open at sixty miles an hour. We all had to pull him and the door back with haste. It seemed to take an eternity once the train started to slow down and pull into the station and as I knew Reading quite well we would be at the back of the platform and close to the goods yard. The train idled into the station and to get a bit of a head start we began to jump off the moving train. Once we were all off, the jog hastened into a sprint as it seemed half of Oxford fancied a stop off en route. About a hundred were chasing us up the platform and all I could hear was nervous giggling, we all scaled the fence and in to town. I have had better days!

Anon 1.

I have had many good rows at QPR, one good one was when we played Cardiff on a Friday night down the Bush.

A few weeks previous I had fucked my leg playing football and was now on crutches, gutted was an understatement as when I got to the British Queen early doors and we were already a hundred handed and the place was buzzing, I certainly wouldn't be playing up tonight though.

Fast forward to early evening and we had a very respectable two to three hundred lads mobbed up inside and outside the pub, albeit by now under a heavy police presence.

Next thing I knew a coach of Cardiff got stuck in traffic on the Uxbridge Road. Cue everyone charging out the pub to be met with a line of plod with horses and dogs.

I had not seen it too many times with us at QPR but old bill were attacked with flares, bottles bricks etc and were backed off down the road and we used this as the opportunity to break through the cordon and head off down many of the back streets towards the ground.

Fair play to Cardiff they were out and all the way to the ground there were sporadic outbreaks of small ten v ten type of rows.

Being on crutches I was lagging behind whilst everyone else I was with was getting involved further up in front of me, I walked round the corner to see some Cardiff getting the better of some of ours and instinct took over and I wellied a Taff over the head with my crutch causing it to snap in half, trouble is he didn't budge! With that he bottled me round the head and my leg gave way and I hit the deck thinking "Shit I'm in trouble here" luckily for me another little mob of Rangers turned up to stop me from getting a pasting. That was certainly an action packed evening in West London! Thanks anon for that story!

That game against Cardiff was on a Friday night and at that time I had hit a rough time in my life. I had found myself homeless due to my boozing and was now living in a shabby little room above a pub in Teddington, South West London. A couple of my mates had lived there for years and we had some mad and funny times there. It was also quite tragic that we had all ended up in a place like that.

Anyway my old mate who is also another good friend of mine's dad and both are QPR supporters. "W" had not been to see the rangers for a long old time and he decided he wanted to come to the Cardiff game with me and would also be a good chance to get out and about and have a few jars with me. Our other pal also came along for the hell of it. We got the tube from Richmond up to Hammersmith and when we came out onto the Broadway we literally bumped into a huge mob of older geezers and were all dressed up in Stone Island clobber. They looked like they would have taken some shifting if I am to be honest.

I said to "W" that this must be one of Cardiff's firms and they were on their way to the Bush. We jumped on a Hammersmith and City Line tube to Shepherds Bush and came out by the market. For a Friday night the Uxbridge Road was packed and it looked like there would be a good attendance this evening. I had planned to take the lads along to the British Queen pub where most of our lot met up these days.

We got down as far as Loftus Road and the road had been blocked off by old bill, they were not letting anyone go any further.

We were all gasping for another ale and I tried sneaking through to get to the Queen, the copper knew me by surname as this was before 2004 when I got sober and started to behave myself.

"Go down there and I'm nicking you, there has been some serious disorder and there is no access for anyone".

My first reaction was that I was gutted that I had missed it all, and now "W" was well pissed off he couldn't get a beer.

"I'm never coming with you again" he stated he came all this way and the old bill know you by name and he was thirsty as an old camel in the Sahara desert.

We eventually got up to the Springbok pub by the ground which was always about six deep at the bar and took about twenty minutes to get served! We ended up staying in the pub and all went back to Teddington again as "W" was in a terrible mood. Just as well, as we lost the game 4-0 just to rub salt in our wounds.

Anonymous 2. I was eighteen in 1982, a great time to be a QPR fan. It was the promotion season and we had a cracking team. In Hayes we had a good sized group of us, at the time we drank in the Brookhouse pub. It was always mobbed from Thursday through to Sunday with like minded lads all dressed in the latest clobber we could get our hands on. There was a mix of QPR, Gooners, West Ham, Chelsea and the odd Spurs fans. We were all from Hayes, we drank together and even holidayed together. Nineteen of us got deported from Rhodes in 1984, that is another story! We were all working class lads enjoying life to the full. They were great times to be alive. When Hayes played in the FA Cup, there was always a great mob, and many a team including Cardiff and Swansea underestimated us at their peril. Getting on to our rangers lot, we used to go through Northolt on our way to the Bush. We formed a good bond with the lads from there, who to this day are good mates. We still see each other at rangers games. We had a mixture of blaggers and thieves, there was always a bit of weed or speed about. Cambridge away in 1982 we were running around the sports and menswear shops helping ourselves! We developed a few rangers related blags around that time. This included tickets at home games being thrown from South Africa Road upper tier and being used again lol. We also used to jib (bunk) our way up and down the country following the R's, when we used to win away games! On top of the usual jibs from mainline London stations, we used to travel early from Northolt through Wycombe and into Birmingham New Street and we paid nothing! Then we went onwards to various shitholes in the Midlands and North. We used that route right through 1982 and 83. There was always a mix of Hayes, Northolt and Greenford lads, not massive numbers but a tidy firm who all knew each other well. A stand out game for us Hayes lot was Derby away in late December 1982. It was just the Hayes lads that day, there was a lot of beer and smoke that day! We got to New

Street as usual without paying and saw a massive lot of Leeds who were playing in Birmingham. We went on to Derby and it went off on the way to the ground. After the game we were ambushed by a big mob of Derby coming from all sides. We made it back to the station and as we came down the platform stairs there was another mob of Derby on the platform and train. It went off big time, I remember a well known ginger haired Hayes lad picking me up off the floor at one stage! Our mate Lester RIP got a nasty slash and ended up in Derby hospital. It was an eventful day and we were back at WBA away in the FA Cup a couple of days later. QPR had a great lot of dressers also from the Bush and we knocked about with the Feltham lot who we initially met at the Monday night disco in the Airman pub, also another story!

"R".

For me Portsmouth at home was naughty when they were in our seats and it kicked off which resulted in the game being stopped, that was a mad one. Wolves one year was another hairy one. We had a proper off with about a hundred and fifty of their Yam Yam army down Uxbridge Road led by their top boy Gilly who I actually became good pals with over the years but the one that really stands out was probably the row with Cardiff City's Soul Crew at home one Friday night in the dark. Now that was a proper battle. There was a massive mob of us in the British Queen pub and Cardiff's boys knew that. They diverted their coaches to stop by the pub a couple of hours before the game thinking they would give it to us but there as one of the biggest Rangers firms out that night with some proper faces in attendance and once the roar went up that they'd arrived it was absolute mayhem. There were pitched battles all over the streets, really vicious stuff. This went on all night. After the game a mob of us were in the now shut down Goldhawk Pub on Goldhawk Rd when someone ran in saying two mini busses of Cardiff's top lads had waited until the OB had fucked off and were slapping Rangers fans. Little did they know we were literally across the road. About forty of us steamed out and caught them cold giving it to some lads by the petrol station. All I'll say is they got an almighty hiding that night, a really bad battering leaving some of them hospitalized in a bad way. Those that were there know who they are and what went down but we'll leave it there. They definitely went back to South Wales with their tails between their legs that night. I spoke to a couple of their proper lads a year or so later after meeting them in a rave in East London and they said they openly admitted between themselves they got a proper serving up that night and although QPR are not the biggest firm in the world they have a hardcore of about sixty to seventy that could mix it with absolutely anyone and they met them that night.

Anon 3.

We all ventured into the North bank Arsenal in 1983 and got involved in a bit of a melee at the bottom of the North bank, there were about thirty of us brave souls. We all got led around the pitch and escorted out, we won 2-0 and we missed everything! We all blamed Irish Pat, I can't remember why? But I think he wanted us to be" brave" as he put it!

Nicky.

It was 1983, I was a ten year old with my older cousin standing on the Loft and watching it kick off after our last game v Wolves. There were running battles on the pitch with police horses. The sound of the roar you hear when it is going off always sounds the same no matter what year it is. It sucks you in and the buzz is born. I couldn't wait for the next, our first season in the old Division One. The first match was against Aston Villa and it went off in the seats. I remember just smiling and wanting to see more. By the time I was twelve I had started going in the paddock with my school mate. We noticed that was where all the dressers went and I started noticing what they wearing. The paddock was just by the away end and I remember Forest coming in there and the terrace opened up. Both set of lads were going toe to toe. By the age of thirteen to fourteen I was starting to get some clothes to look like a casual. I had a few hand me downs from my cousin and normally Christmas presents and my dad shaking his head and looking on in horror as he had he just bought me a pair of Lois jeans. I put a slit down the sides, it always makes me laugh and me telling him that's what casuals do still make me laugh. By time I was fifteen or sixteen a few of us younger lot would meet up early on a Saturday morning and go to the Bush Ranger pub. By now some of the older lads started to notice us and I remember Gregor giving me a pep talk about my pink jumper on the way to Oxford saying are you willing to stand out today. I'd say from 1983-90 you'd often see fighting in the ground as well as in the streets. There have been loads but I remember the Rangers and Leicester Baby squad in the BBC park and then again with Leicester in the cup in the Ellerslie Road stand. That was a proper old school row at half time. Forest always was good, home or away and not forgetting Norwich, Ipswich and Oxford had good firms around this time. A good ground to go to and get a row was Southampton's The Dell. We went in their seats one year and they weren't pleased but they couldn't move us. I remember we tried the same move at Spurs a couple of weeks later but we didn't get the same result and got marched around the pitch as the old bill nicked me and a few others they let us go at the gate. This was after letting the Spurs lads who didn't go in to the game know we were Rangers and we got some looks but they gave us a squeeze as there were only four of us. We had some scary moments and went home reliving the day over again and smiling. I have seen so called big teams get turned over but also seen us come unstuck, that's football. 1983-90 was my favourite era as we had a decent team and a firm that could hold our own.

1990 started with Cardiff City away, now this was the youths away day my seventeenth birthday. This is one I'll never forget, there must have been about twenty of us. I think we went on the train and didn't realize how big this game was to them. Until last year when I was chatting to a Cardiff lad and he told me that was when Cardiff started really getting it together and he wasn't lying. As we got off the train opposite the old Wimpy burger bar, hundreds of Cardiff came marching towards us. We could see the old bill was shitting it and pushed us in the station. Believe me getting to the ground was up there with the scariest football away days with fighting breaking all over the place. After a 0-0 draw a lot of revenge was dished out back at Rangers with Cardiff lads getting slapped and the same Cardiff lad admitted it came on top for them in the replay. The 1990s was I'd say the beginning of the end as football wasn't the main thing for young lads any more. The rave scene was here, I remember going to Energy, Raindance, Sunrise and many more and football became secondary. Lads came together from different clubs from all over the country and got to know each other, but it's not to say it never kicked off every now and again. I still went to Norwich, Luton, Forest and Southampton and a couple more. Rangers would always go there but the numbers wasn't like years before. A game that stands out from the mid 90s must be Portsmouth at home for some reason the 657 made this their big game. It was massive, and I mean massive, they got into the

Ellerslie seats and I was smack bang in the middle of them. Me and my mate Walshy, it was a long forty five minutes as they knew we was Rangers. By halftime fighting had broken out in most parts of the ground with it even making the news. I never lost the buzz but it wasn't the same as the rows were getting less and less, but there was always a chance it might go off. Such as Sheffield United where I saw my pal get nicked for throwing a water melon and he got a ban for it. I remember Grimsby having a go at one night game when their lad had gas but ended up gassing himself as the nozzles must have been the wrong way round. He took a few slaps for being stupid lol. Leeds also stood out as they admit they took us lightly that night and got done in Wormholt Park. Coventry was always that team that would surprise us, maybe I was just unlucky. Two teams around this time that was always tasty was Stoke and Port Vale. Port Vale are game at home but can't really remember them coming to us whereas Stoke will entertain home or away. By the early 2000s I had other interests and by now we had a shit team and not many lads could be bothered anymore. I remember walking through White City on my way home when I got chatting to a young lad I'd noticed at Rangers but never talked. His name was Lee who lived on the estate, anyway a couple of weeks or so later Rangers was at Coventry's Highfield Road. He told me the youth was going and if I wanted to come as I hadn't been there before I thought I would go. On that day I saw the Rangers youth in action, they done well and took it to Coventry and got a result and finally I can say Rangers got one over my bogey team. The buzz was back and Rangers started turning out more often between the years of 2005 and 2010. We had some good rows, especially with Millwall and a good pal from South London who if he reads this would know who he is. He tells me that he loved playing us, especially at night and I was starting to have more luck away at Coventry than I ever had at Loftus Road. QPR turned Coventry over at their first game at the Ricoh. At this time Rangers we're making a name for themselves going to places like Villa, Bristol City, Millwall etc and no longer fearing the so-called bigger firms but the old bill brought top spotters and soon bans were starting to be dished out. They needed to break us up, a few youth lads got bans and even prison for rows and then we had an old school row with Bristol City at the old British Queen pub which for certain reasons I won't go into. But if you were there you know what happened and within a couple of months I was hit with a three year ban. And to be honest that was the end for me as by now I had a son and wanted to bring him to the matches. I have been back to Millwall and it still always draws out and of course our old foes Luton. They are my favourite team home or away. I hate them but respect and rate them as they are like us, not the biggest but will mix it with the big boys and get results. So I've saved my best one till last, St Pancras. For some reason there are some you remember more than others but I remember it kicking off early doors with them around midday. We used to sit in the Ellerslie Road stand, just by the away end and we'd get in the ground around 3.10 so the away teams lads knew you was there. About ten or so Luton was in our end who got chased out on to the pitch. Nothing really happened after the game as we walked the streets looking for the MIGS as this was pre mobile phone era. There was no way of contacting them, so we knew that Luton would go back to St. Pancras station. We all got on the train and when we got off, I remember there was Arsenal across the platform and I think the Gooner's thought EIE as they was known for saying. But they didn't make a move when Fat Pat who was Chelsea and a good lad and became a good mate with us. We came down that slope by the station saying the MIGS are in there we walked with no noise, then when in the station the roar went up and Luton started to run. They got broom sticks but were overrun and got a severe beating with some of them running down the tracks. I got nicked a few weeks later due to my deerstalker hat. Shit happens lol. Respect to all the Rangers lads past and present who I've shared laughs with of being a football lad and RIP to Jon Jon he always told us an old school story on an away day. Also Streatham Steve, he was always laughing and Fat Pat from Chelsea saved my skin against Boro on the Goldhawk Road and up at Blackpool. He was a good mate and always had time for a chat. Let's not forget the Swansea jacks, always made me feel welcome also a shout to West Ham Sam, a funny fucker always makes me smile. The DLF Derby, I got to know some good lads from there. Also to the Millwall boys, you know who you are respect to you lads.

M.

These are some accounts from a fella who wishes only to be known as "M". These games were from the late 1990's and early 2000's I believe.

As I stated before I had four banning orders over the years and a lot of these matches I missed out on.

Port Vale away. QPR were in League One (Championship), the team were on a downward spiral and heading for relegation. It was in the late 1990's unsure of the exact season. M says it was one of those "must go to" games as before the corresponding fixture the season before three of our good lads took a bad beating in a bookies shop and were badly outnumbered. It was a bit of liberty taken by Vale but as we all know shit happens but it still doesn't make it right. About 150-200 turned out for this and all met up in some pub, which the name escapes M. There was no trouble before the game.

Just before the game an "army" of hundreds of Vale's mob entered the ground to the left of the away end. When the rangers scored loads of our lot spilled onto the pitch with the usual goading of the home fans with loads of eyeing up and verbals. The old bill got heavy handed and pushed back the QPR lads and began whacking out with their batons. M says the atmosphere throughout was very nasty indeed!

After the game most of the R's headed to a massive car park where there were coaches parked, some of the lads had driven up, some by train and some coaches, but they were all together. Port Vales boys attacked in great numbers and there were about two hundred geezers literally having a free for all in this car park. M says there were bods rolling over car bonnets and even saw a couple of lads diving underneath a coach to get away. M was grabbed by a copper round his throat and took a whack from a baton and shoved into an old bill wagon. M says he tried to kick back to no avail.

M thought he was being nicked for sure but thankfully was taken straight back to the train station. Unluckily though, he had come up in a motor with a few others and had to make his way back to the car and to near the scene of all the trouble. M was on his lonesome and said it was a very hairy experience making it back in one piece! M's legs were swollen right up and it was a very painful journey home.

Wolves away. Again unsure of the exact year. M remembers that the week or two before, one of the top Football Intelligence officers had been decked at Huddersfield away. Only fifteen or twenty of M's crowd headed up on the rattler to Birmingham and then into Wolverhampton. A lot of chaps will tell you that not many little mobs ever venturied before the game to go drinking in Wolverhampton, most stay in Brum and then head in to the game. So fair play for going into no mans land!

They found a pub which already had a lot of QPR's shirters in there. The FIU officer walked in with his merry men and a lot of the lads began winding him up about the incident at Huddersfield. He was not happy to say the least. They were all escorted to the ground.

After the match ended the FIU took the lads as far as the infamous subway and left them there and went their own way. Within a minute or two about thirty of Wolves finest appeared and a few of the R's lads took a spanking. A few tried to hold their own. M says he lost half of a tooth to a very good right hander. They had to retreat and found some ammunition in the form of builders' rubble which was fired back as they made their way down an alleyway back to a main street and to safety.

On the train home all the lads were comparing war wounds from their onslaught and were having a good laugh about it.

M is convinced that the FIU officer had stitched them right up as he had the right hump and left them to fend for themselves at the subway.

Peterbrough away. Early 2000's. M says nothing had

happened before the game and afterwards was in the pub right opposite the train station. There was only about seven or eight lads together. A Peterborough bod walked in and announced "Do you lot want it?" The rangers chaps explained there was only eight of them. This didn't matter to the Posh boys as it didn't take long before they arrived back with a good thirty of them and all very keen. Luckily for the hateful eight another thirty QPR on their way back for the train had seen what was going on and let's just say the brave Peterborough mob ran like a pack of Usain Bolts. M says two or three of them were cornered in the station car park and were pleading with some old bill for help! Just desserts was served.

Hull City away. Early 2000's mid 2000's? Hull fans had been taunting the QPR fans by chanting "You're just a town full of bombers" following terrorist attacks on the buses and tube trains in London. Obviously this pissed off the R's firm that was there. Outside the ground after the match QPR tried to get at the Hull lot and a wire fence was pushed over with coins being thrown. There was a scuffle or two. QPR have hated Hull even more since that match. This is an account from another lad who was there; We were going at them in their stadium and then took it outside. We came out and a load of blokes jumped from parked cars and started throwing stones at us. My mate said you "wanna stone fight!"! And that was it, we battered all of them. It was a good turn out.

Lee.

Here's a story that happened to me and my mates about 1986. I was eighteen and going to QPR, I think it was against Newcastle United and we had just parked our car and were walking towards the pub when my mate wanted a piss. So he went into a bush and had a piss. We had walked on and he was followed by about four or five geordies and they jumped him and literally kicked the shit outta him. He managed to get to the pub and was talking to us describing the guys. Then ten rangers fans walked out of the pub. They were gone for about ten minutes and came back and said to my mate "no worries son, problem sorted!"

I went to the league cup game against Crewe we won 8-1. After the game, I was walking to the station and got jumped by some Crewe fans .I was about fifteen at the time and was just swinging my arms about like a lunatic. I managed to get away and meet my mates at the station, then a Crewe fan wanted my mates scarf to wipe his arse on. I said to fuck yourself that's my mate's, if you want one go. But one of them swung for me and missed. I just kicked him in the bollocks and needless to say he didn't get up!

"**Mick**"

Stoke away, after they built their Britannia stadium, it was a night game, we was all firmed up. We got run but re-grouped and had it in some waste land. That was mad. Brentford away. A handful got run and I was in a local pub and then my mucker came down with about 150 youth. Three pubs got demolished. (this was 2001 a midday kick off) the Ealing Gazette reported that several hours after the match, a large group of QPR fans came back to the pubs around Griffin Park. There was some skirmishing in the streets and a couple of pubs were smashed up. There were two arrests. QPR v Palace, early 2000's on the Bush green, QPR were coming at all angles and all they could do was hide behind the old bill. Needless to say Palace have done well at ours on other occasions.

The same lad also says "We always say that if Ladbroke Grove, Bush, Acton, Ealing, Harlesden, Kensal Rise, Northolt, Hanwell, Eastcote, Ruislip Hayes and Greenford got together we would have had a mad firm.

We have too many factions. I have seen too many arguments between the rangers."

Bill Preston North End:

When QPR came to ours earlier in the season, half a dozen of us fourteen to fifteen year olds were hanging around outside Deepdale trying to jump the turnstiles. All of a sudden two big blokes, one wearing a donkey jacket with a big scar across his boat race, beckoned us on. They must have been ten years older than us and had intent wrote all over their faces. Us younguns weren't sizable enough yet to take on grown men. We did a bit of dancing before the coppers arrived and we did one.

My second visit to London was in 1980, to Loftus Road, the home of QPR, the R's. I was getting older, but not necessary wiser. I travelled with my two mates. This time with an air of anxiety not cocksure like the last when I went to Stamford Bridge.

We arrived early after making good time on the same pub coach. The scarfers and the flask brigade go straight on to the half-developed ground, two sides had seats installed, elevated over the existing terracing, a really weird sight. Us three rascals fancied a bit of a shifty about, so we went for walkies.

On our travels we walked pass the famous White City greyhound track in a stage of being knocked down. I suppose more high-rise flats were needed for the ever growing London population. The area surrounding the track was already saturated in cold eerie concrete tenant blocks. This being a perfect location for an ambush, a nightmare place when getting chased, losing your way and getting trapped in dead-ends.

The season before, a coach when pulling away from the ground, had come under attack getting the majority of its windows put through. Lads had jumped through shattered, glass windows and the emergency door, trying to catch the perpetrators who disappear quicker than they appeared. A cold trip home was had with lads cursing through chattering teeth.

We reached a mini-spaghetti junction with smog rising and noise bouncing off all the man made structures. There was hardly a blade of grass to be seen. We eventually found a large public house, Smuts or summat, which we entered.

We were seemingly transported Tardis fashion to a Jamaican beach bar without the beach? We'd only taken a couple of steps inside when the bloke behind the bar shouted over, "You boys will get a drink in the other side."

Fifty pairs of brown eyes were focusing on us. We did an about turn, doing as we're told, turning left, into the other side. This side of the pub was full of geezers wearing QPR tops and scarves. We order three lagers and sit ourselves down at a table near the dartboard. Two pubs in Preston, the Bull & Royal and Red Lion had similar clientele, but not to this extent. A South African apartheid feel, very surreal. We sup our pints slowly until the home fans made a move with us following suit not wanting to outstay our welcome.

After paying onto the open away end, once more Preston had a sparse, thinly spread following. "I never felt more like singing the blues" was being played over the tannoy system. In with North End, were a few QPR lads dotted about. They were whistling away to their song, letting each other know they're in, willing and waiting.

Preston never took a mob, or a firm, and I started wondering why I bothered travelling, just where were the rest?

Heading home on the coach later, I mulled over if it was worth all the mileage just to watch a game. Of course it was! I'm following Preston North End, the best team the world has ever seen, ha!

6 THE 1990'S

I would like to give a mention to Brighton who always seemed to show in big numbers to us in the 1990's. I can't remember the exact year but after one home game at Loftus Road I went for a few beers in Hammersmith after the game. A load of us would always head back to the Wetherspoons "The George" in King Street. There was also a Belushi's right on the Broadway.

After that particular game I was sitting in Belushi's with about ten or so of the regular faces. I was supposed to be meeting my missus over in Gunnersbury for a meal with her brother. I was already late as I was getting right involved with the lads as you do.

We had been in there about an hour when all of a sudden

about three lads with their hoods pulled up came to the main window beckoning us out.

Well, when I saw that it was like waving a red flag to a bull and I was straight out of the door in pursuit of my Matadors. I didn't even look back to see who had followed me.

It is a fair distance to chase three blokes right up the Broadway to where the Hammersmith Apollo is. I thought I had done the biz and chased them off until I turned the corner to be met by about thirty very game looking chaps. They were probably a lot younger than myself at the time and the lad at the front had taken off his belt and came toward me swinging it like a lassoo. I only then looked behind me to see that only one other of my fellow R's had joined me in pursuit of our hooded pals.

To be fair I had to retreat sharpishly, and when I had a skin full of booze I hated running from anyone. The odds were well against us here so I ran backwards so I was facing them, and I certainly didn't want a belt buckle smashed over the back of my nut. By the time I got back to Belushi's there was the all familiar sound of old bill sirens. They must have been alerted or had been given the heads up that there was a firm on the large looking for it around Hammersmith. It turned out that it was a little mob of Brighton Youth who had been playing up the road at Fulham.

The other rangers lot in the pub were now all outside although being held back now by the law. The Brighton lot decided to turn back and get out of trouble.

So, that all ended before anything had really started. I called my other half and told her what had just happened and that I wanted to stay out a bit longer as we were going to bump into the Brighton a bit later. She went ballistic and insisted I got to Gunnersbury as her brother was now there and the dinner was going to be late. I reluctantly jumped on a District Line tube and ended up having a really good evening.

I was a bit gutted as I found out the next day that QPR had found the Brighton mob down Fulham Palace Road later and gave them a good hiding.

Another time when we were playing Brighton, again around the mid-late 1990's it was one of those tin pot cup games and I am sure it was a Sunday lunchtime kick-off.

I was with one of the old school geezers that morning and

we met early and had a couple of pints up in Hammersmith before heading to the Bush. As I write this book I have had the very sad news that my old mate has passed away only yesterday. RIP George, you were a diamond and I have many great and funny moments with you at QPR and when we were out and about for a good piss-up back in the day before I got sober.

Myself and George got off at Goldhawk Road station and decided to get a quick one in the British Prince next door. As we walked in the door the whole bar was full of what I would describe as Brighton's main firm of older heads.

To be fair they looked a right handful, we whispered to each other that we either do one out the door and bring it on top for ourselves or just keep calm and carry on ordering a pint at the bar. We went for the latter and got our drinks and went and sat down and kind of pretended we were nothing to do with the football that day.

We didn't stay too long but for sure the Brighton lads did look us over and I think they knew were QPR, but we kept it low key.

We went up to the Adelaide along Uxbridge Road and there

was only handful of our lads in there. We hardly had anyone out that day so Brighton probably said they came that day with no show from us which is fair to be honest.

I reckon they had shown that day following a massive row that occurred outside the Richmond Arms along the Shepherds Bush Road a season or two before. Loads had been nicked for that one from both sides, and that was another one that I missed out on.

This is a newspaper article and I am unsure from which paper or the date;

"Organized football hooliganism reared its ugly head during a pre-arranged fight in the George pub, Hammersmith between QPR, Chelsea and Brighton fans.

After an earlier planned skirmish had been successfully averted at Craven Cottage as Albion went down 2-0 to Fulham. Groups of known troublemakers appear to have set up a second punch-up which resulted in four arrests. One of the arrested was charged with carrying a CS gas canister.

Dozens of passers by ran to avoid being caught up in the fight which started at 6pm- just over an hour after the Fulham game ended.

Detective Chief Inspector "DK" of Hammersmith Police was adamant that the fight which spilled on to the Broadway and then onto the road was pre-arranged.

He said "our intelligence picked out known troublemakers from QPR and Chelsea". One of the so called QPR fans has just been able to return to Loftus Road after a three year exclusion order. It certainly appears that these men weren't in the pub by chance, especially as some of them were not local.

One man from Tooting and two from Brighton have been charged under Section 4 of the Public Order Act while another from Putney was cautioned.

Fulham director "AM" had warned him of a possible riot at Fulham's game.

He said "We knew something had been planned. That's why we were particularly vigilant during the game about our own security arrangements.

"The last thing we want to attract because of our current success is this sort of element. It seems sad that his sort of throwback is obviously there under the surface. I only hope it is dealt with vigorously".

During the match itself police had to move into the Brighton section at the Bishop's Park end of the ground and eject several travelling supporters after Brighton had missed a penalty during the first half.

7 FULHAM 1999 A CONSPIRACY THEORY

QPR had not played our local neighbours from up the other end of Fulham Palace Road since 1983, the year we were promoted to the old First Division. Chelsea has always been our biggest enemy but to put one over the boys in white is always very satisfying.

Fulham had fallen down the divisions and now had a new chairman at the helm. Al Fayed the owner of Harrods had started to pump his money into the club and they were on their way back up. So in the season 1999/2000 we were both back in the same division. We were to play at Craven Cottage in September 99.

I had just been on a holiday to Faliraki in Rhodes a Greek Island with my then first wife. I lived in Catford at the time and a lot of the lads at the R's especially our own little crowd gave me the nickname "Catford". A couple of the lads in our group were both from south as well, Stockwell and Brixton.

This was one of those games that everyone wanted to go to, there just wasn't enough tickets on sale to go around. I myself was unable to get a ticket but have had success in the past in getting one from a fellow QPR fan in a pub on the day. I decided there was no way I was missing out on this game, and even if I couldn't get a ticket at least I would meet up with the lads for the laugh.

I arranged with my lot to meet in the Golden Gloves pub (new name Suffolk Punch) along the Fulham Palace Road. All the pubs were full with QPR fans early doors that day. I even remember what I was wearing, I had a new blue chequed Lacoste short sleeve shirt, jeans and a blue Nike baseball cap. As usual there was a lot of Stone Island on show that day from the other fellas.

There was a brilliant buzz in the pub and I saw loads of faces and mates from my old days back in Teddington from my youth. I had a decent sun tan from Faliraki and was feeling on top of the world. It was every man for himself trying to get hold of a match ticket. Eventually I found out that someone had a mate from Fulham who had got hold of a load of tickets for their side terrace the Stevenage Road stand. At first I was a bit dubious and at that time I was well known to the Football Intelligence Unit who was always lurking nearby. I got a ticket and told myself to just keep my head down in the ground and not get in any bother.

The usual old bill vans were parked across the road from the pub and were obviously filming and taking stills of fans.

Then came that moment when we decided to take a walk to the ground, the excitement of how the game would go and the hope of winning and beating the locals for the first time in sixteen years.

The streets were packed and there were herds of QPR fans all over the place.

As I walked up to the Stevenage Road turnstile which is right next to the away end I could see about ten of the older lot that I know well entering the same stand as me. A few nods of heads and in we went. My heart was pounding as we made our way through the masses of Fulham fans and on to the terrace in the lower tier. The whole ground was packed solid and the atmosphere was building up nicely. I stuck close by my rangers counterparts and we all stood in a line right at the back of the terrace. Heads were turning and it was obvious that the locals knew we were QPR. As it is at every ground up and down the country, you just know when a group walks in that you have never seen before. A lot of these lads are well known over the years anyway, and Fulham isn't exactly a million miles away from us!

There were about five minutes to go until kick off and one of our lot started up a song... "Oh when the R's" and before he got to the "go marching in" part a punch had already been thrown. That was the cue for bedlam, I just remember being dragged down the terrace, I was well pissed up and not in total control of senses at that point. I turned to my left and saw some huge lump coming toward me, my self defense mode kicked in and stood my ground with my arms stretched out. I was totally unaware of what else was going on around me. Back in my drinking days I was a loose cannon to say the least and as I ended up against the perimeter wall by the pitch I kept facing the hundreds of home fans surging toward us baying for our blood. It all had happened so quickly and I honestly could not tell you the finer details of what happened in those twenty seconds of madness. Someone grabbed hold of my shirt and literally ripped me off the terrace and on to the pitch. I thought I had been nicked and I was frog marched away toward the QPR end. I saw some of our lads climbing back in to the away end and to freedom. It then became clear that I was not going to be allowed back in with my own fans. I pleaded with my captor to let me go but he carted me off down the players' tunnel. We got to a big exit door and I was thrown out onto the street outside. There were still hundreds of fans still queuing to get in.

I couldn't believe it when Gregor came running over and stood in front of me. I told him that it had all just kicked off, and he pointed out to me that my shirt was ripped open and there was only a couple of buttons still left intact.

"Tuck yourself in mate" Gregor said and to be honest I was just waiting to be nicked. That never happened but a couple of old bill came over and told us to fuck off away. Gregor was adamant he was waiting for a ticket from someone but the coppers were having none of it and said we would be in the back of a van if we didn't move sharpish.

I was still well drunk and all I could think about now was getting another pint from somewhere. The lad I knew from

Brixton was with Gregor and also did not manage to get hold of a ticket and he said he knew of a pub just up the road. We headed up to the boozer and as we entered the door, the guvnor said he was closing and we couldn't come in. I pleaded with him to sell us a bottle to take away, and we managed to get a bottle each except for Gregor who I have never seen drink at football in my life. We were charged about a fiver each which was a total piss-take at the time, but needs must!

We hung around near the ground and just generally chatted about shit until about twenty minutes before the end of the match I decided to go for a walk up to the Palace Road on my own. Then it dawned on me that I wanted to meet up with all my mates in the ground again and headed back to the ground.

As both sets of fans left the ground, a massive old bill presence did their best to separate us from Fulham, apparently there had been more incidents in the ground in nearly every stand. It was like the 1980's all over again except the police had it pretty much under control. I was pleased to see my mates who were in the away end, they were pissing themselves that they saw me being led round the pitch and thrown out.

A lot more offs were occurring all over the place but I just wanted to get out of there and head back to Hammersmith or the Bush for a couple more pints. I was skint by now otherwise I would have stayed out all night and got ruined.

I went back to Catford that night with an open shirt and minus my baseball cap which had flown off during the melee in the Fulham terracing. I explained to my Mrs at the time what had happened and she was very concerned. I said it was all ok or I would have been nicked there and then surely.

The trouble was all over the Sunday tabloids the next day and on the Monday I went back to work. On the train home I picked up a copy of the Evening Standard which had an article about how the Met Police and Football Intelligence were now studying CCTV footage and were confident of making arrests. This got me a bit worried but I was convinced I had not really done anything too bad. I had been attacked in the Fulham end and was just defending myself. I was proper paralytic though and in a mild black-out about the events.

About a month went by and one afternoon I was at work and I had a mobile phone, this was still fairly early days for mobiles and computers. My great pal N rang me and told me he had been spoken to by the FIU at our game that weekend. I deliberately had stayed away for that month as I wanted to keep a low one. There had already been quite a lot of nickings from both sides and it was known that Gregor was one of them and was already on remand. Some of our lads had been dealt with quickly and had been charged for minor public order offences.

Anyway my mate N told me that one of the officers that knew me at QPR wanted met o give them a call at Fulham station. I rang them and they asked me to come in for questioning, either that or they were going to bust my door down one early morning. I was just grateful they had not already paid me a visit and caused a scene down my road in Catford, I had been trying to keep out of trouble since I moved away from my old manor.

I seriously thought I had not too much to worry about and arranged for my missus to come with me one afternoon after work. We were going to go for a meal after my visit to the old bill. I made one fatal mistake, I did not bother getting a brief to represent me. I was questioned by a detective sergeant who was not Football Intelligence. Lets just say he was like the Gestapo, he tried winding me up so I got angry during the interview. I didn't bite, in hindsight I should have just gone "no comment" but I just explained that I got a ticket for the Fulham end and was attacked when they realized we were QPR. This was pretty much the truth anyway.

The DS was raging, he accused me of being a total liar and that he knew it was all planned and I was being charged with conspiracy to cause violent disorder. I had already been banned from football and done a short prison sentence for my stupidity. I was always pissed and had no boundaries. He then went on to tell me I wasn't getting bail, I was being held until the morning and being taken to West London Magistrates. Gutted wasn't the word, my poor wife was outside and had to make her way back to Catford without me.

I had been in nick seven times before and I really thought I had seen the back of prison back in 1992 the last time I was inside.

The next day at court I arranged to see a duty solicitor and ran the whole story by him. He even agreed that a conspiracy charge seemed well harsh, he was going to try and get me bailed with the conditions of a financial surety. The only person that could possibly help me with that was my wife's brother who had a decent job and had never been in any bother before.

Fair play to my brief he got me bail but I would not be let out until the surety was secured. I waited all afternoon and had to go to HMP Wandsworth that evening as it was too late. Another shitty journey in a sweat box and in through the famous wooden gates of Wanno prison. I spent the night in there and all my horrible memories of serving time came flooding back to me.

Breakfast came and went the next morning and I was sure I would be out by ten am. This didn't happen so I was now certain that my surety could not be raised by my bro in law. The clunk of the heavy metal door opened up with a screw standing there, this was it surely. "Exercise" he announced, my jaw must have dropped, but I went out for a morning walk anyway to take my mind off things. As I got out onto the courtyard and started walking round with the other inmates, Gregor came running over. He seemed well chuffed to see me. I told him I was waiting for bail and it was his turn to look gutted, even though he was probably pleased for me anyway. We spoke a bit about the case and how ridiculous the charge of conspiracy was, Gregor had done fuck all and I had just been pissed as usual in the line of fire.

Just before lunchtime I was let out of the prison, it was a nice sunny day and I walked up to Earlsfield station and got the train back to Waterloo and on to Catford. My missus obviously was not happy. I had done really well in staying out of trouble for a good few years. This was just a day of excitement that went wrong.

Another of my mates, Tony had also been nicked for a separate incident in the seats above the terrace where it had all kicked off. Tony recommended me a very good law firm that had previous dealings with football related cases in Crown Court. I met with them in their chambers in Temple up near Embankment . They seemed to know their stuff, they said they now had a video of all the CCTV footage which went on for about three hours and was taken from all angles in and outside the ground.

When I had been questioned by the DS at Fulham he had

shown me some photos of me and some others standing outside the pub and I was talking on my mobile phone. He tried to make out that I was arranging violence at the match which was bullshit. Another camera shot showed me inside the ground with a couple of stewards holding me back with my arm raised up toward the Fulham fans who had been charging at me. I told the barrister I was just defending myself, which I was, but I was pissed so that didn't help matters. Most of the other lads had just tried to get out of there and back in to the away end. Booze has always been my demon, which I will go into later in this book.

We had a pre-trial hearing at West London magistrates and the other lads who had been nicked were there. My barrister suggested I plead guilty to a charge of threatening behaviour as the CCTV evidence did me no justice. I agreed and the conspiracy charges were dropped on all of us. This was a massive relief as it carried a very long prison sentence. And the courts were clamping down on football violence cases and there was an ongoing case with some Chelsea lads, which included an old mate of mine from my old manor Jason M and Andy F. Tony had told me that the DS in charge of our case was also involved in the Chelsea case.

Our hearing was to take place at Marylebone Magistrates, for what reason I do not know. To cut a long story short, Tony and Gregor had their cases thrown out and myself and MM pleaded guilty to the lesser charge and received massive fines and a three year ban. It was luckily I was not banged up again to be honest so I took that on the chin. I hated being banned it is a pain in the arse but surely better than being locked up again.

This is Tony H's account of that whole episode;

The 18th September 1999 is a day I don't think I'll ever forget. The last time we played Fulham was in 1983, the year we won the old second division and whilst we, albeit for a short time went on to bigger and better things, they plummeted down the divisions and we never saw them again, until now. In the footballing bubble of West London this game was a massive local derby and had been hyped up for weeks. In truth, I'd never really understood our rivalry with Chelsea because geographically speaking Fulham was our closest rival and in order to get to Stamford Bridge we'd have to pass by Craven Cottage which kind of goes against the spirit of local rivalries. By the same token though Chelsea's rivals should really be Fulham but they couldn't have cared less for their nearest neighbour and it's fair to say we weren't on their radar either. I think this is probably due to the fact they have always been a massive club and apart from in the 80's when they were shit they have always won stuff, so compared to us they have always mixed in more esteemed company. Regardless though for some reason this little, local fixture seemed to be capturing everyone's attention. Even Soccer AM's Tim Lovejoy got in on the act by trying to belittle the occasion, saying how dark it was going to be in West London because of the looming shadow being cast over by his boys from Stamford Bridge.

It seemed that everyone was talking about the game and tickets were very hard to come by as the game was sold out within hours of them going on sale. One of the peculiarities of our West London triangle was despite some denials there was always quite a lot of cooperation between some of the chaps of our three clubs. With Fulham being lower down the divisions, quite often their games would be on the same Saturdays as ours and there were many occasions where if a tasty opposition was playing at Craven Cottage a joint venture between Chelsea, Fulham and QPR would frequently ambush the unlucky opposition around Hammersmith. Two memorable rows that spring to mind would be Brighton and Cardiff so the prospect that there would be any trouble at this game was quite far removed from my mind and there certainly weren't any rumours of such either. A couple of weeks before the game, I got a phone call from N who had some complimentary tickets for Fulham v Charlton. QPR were away that day and I wasn't going so a few of us arranged to meet up, go to the game and see if we could get some tickets for the big game. We also met up with Little D who despite always hanging around with QPR lads is a massive Fulham fan. Now D is a great lad and a good friend but he has always suffered from the fact that he is really a QPR supporter trapped inside the body of a Fulham fan, his Fulham tattoos are just a denial of the truth. It must be pure hell living as a 'trans-fan' but hopefully one day now that we are living in more enlightened and progressive times he can find the courage and come out to reveal his true Super Hoops self. Despite all their new found wealth and big names, the game was boring and Fulham were pretty poor which gave me confidence for September 18th that we wouldn't embarrass ourselves. We left at half time and predictably ended up in a pub, we also didn't score any tickets.

On the day of the game I travelled down with a good crew

from North Herts and headed for Hammersmith. We knew that we'd have a massive firm out today and the main talk was of who we could encounter in London. When we arrived at Hammersmith, the place was heaving and was full of old faces, a real who's who of QPR past and present. A lot of lads who go to football seem to develop a kind of numeracy disorder when estimating firm sizes and quite often twenty lads can somehow be counted as fifty. I have thankfully never been prone to this affliction, but I would estimate that on this day we easily numbered four hundred and is the best QPR turnout I have ever seen numbers wise, (the numerical deficient among our support will probably put us at around one thousand!) We bumped in to R and D two of the gamest lads I've ever known and R informed me he had a spare ticket for the Stevenage Road stand. I took it straight away despite it being one of the home stands. My dad was a Fulham fan and I'd been in there before so it didn't really hold any fears for me and I didn't anticipate any problems. R had also sold another ticket to a mate of his in the same row so at least I knew that I wouldn't be totally alone if it did come on top.

Surprisingly for me I managed to get into the ground about five minutes before kick off. No sooner had I took my seat in the stand, a massive roar went up from the terrace below, I recognized the sound immediately as one associated with a tear-up. I went down to the front of the stand to see a big space open up around a small group who I instantly recognized as QPR chaps. Almost at once and without any clear signal the Fulham fans who had retreated from around this small group of invaders surged towards them and fists started to fly. I looked down from the upper tier and thought that these blokes must be absolutely crazy. What they did was an absolute suicide mission and there was only ever going to be one outcome. It took a whole terrace of Fulham fans to move them out and once they'd escaped they managed to find their way into the QPR end. Once calm had been restored the game was able to commence but the punch up below had highlighted the fact that there were plenty of QPR fans in the Stevenage Road stand and in fact all over Craven Cottage. The atmosphere by now was pretty hostile which is something that I've always enjoyed. One QPR fan who had attracted unwanted attention was I assumed to be R and D's mate who was getting dogs abuse. He just sat there and smiled it all off which seemed to wind them up even more. At one stage we made eye contact and I gave him a knowing nod just to let him know that he wasn't alone. He just nodded back and carried on passively winding up the locals but when the inevitable happened and Fulham scored, several QPR fans got up and started giving off. This incensed the Fulham fans and another punch up was inevitable. The main bulk of QPR fans in the Stevenage Road were over to my left which was where my attention was focused so I didn't notice to my right a group of Fulham fans moving towards R and D's mate to attack him. As they went past me one of them shouted my name and punched me in the side of the head, I immediately punched him back but found myself in the middle of a small group who were all intent on giving me a good kicking. It's very strange but in the situation I was in, my mind was so clear that I instinctively knew to just focus on one of them and despite the punches raining in on me I managed to back them all off. As I moved away from the situation, a woman tripped me up, as I stumbled and fell onto a seat the Fulham lads moved in for the kill. I couldn't see how many were on me but I could feel their footprints on my head and back as I slid off the heavily varnished wooden seat and into the foot space between the seats which probably saved me from a severe beating. The sight of the police turning up made some of them disperse and I was able to get away up the gangway towards the back of the stand. A copper came up and grabbed me and as I stood there presumably under arrest, I received a final punch from behind. At this point one of the QPR football intelligence officers came purposefully striding up the gangway, snatched me away from his colleague and launched me down the stairs into another group of coppers. Whilst in this scrum, I was lifted off my feet and I could feel a gloved hand grabbing and gouging at my face. On the police brutality scale, it was fairly negligible, but it was quite scary to not be in control of your body and roughing up a bloke when you're mob handed isn't really the done thing. Most football lads wouldn't behave like this so why should the police.

Once outside the ground the same football intelligence copper who had taken me away from my rescuing police officer arrested me. The fact that he did this made me come to the realization that I wasn't in a good situation. From that moment on, I started working on my defense. I knew full well that Craven Cottage had CCTV but I asked the arresting officer, who had now been joined by another intelligence officer, if this was the case. He responded with a smile that the ground had excellent CCTV facilities but his smile soon disappeared when I replied that I hoped it did. I then concealed my delight when I noticed him write my words down in his notebook. I was booked into Fulham police station for affray and I again repeated my words that I hoped the ground had CCTV as I had been battered. I spoke with my solicitor who represented a lot of football lads and was well known to Fulham old bill especially as he had a lot of regular clients from Chelsea, QPR and Reading to name but a few. I did expect to be held all night and interviewed, so was pleasantly surprised to be released on bail after only a couple hours. I desperately wanted to get back to the pub but before I could do that my survival instinct kicked in and I headed to casualty at Charing Cross hospital to get my injuries checked out. I only had a few cuts and bruises but from the second I had been arrested I was building my case and a trip to A and E which would be documented could only help. When I eventually got back to Hammersmith everyone had a story to tell about what had happened and it appeared that all the good stuff had happened after the final whistle and what had gone on before had just been the warm up. I was gutted to have missed it all because the highlight of my day had been to sit on a foam mattress and read an abridged version of the police custody codes of practice.

When I got back to Kings Cross to catch my train home I bumped into a couple of young Hertfordshire Chelsea lads that I knew. They'd had a bit of grief with a lone jock and asked me to sort him out. I didn't really want to get involved in anything else but I reluctantly obliged. As I walked up to him I saw the fear in his face and immediately knew that I couldn't just chin him. I asked him what his problem was and he just said he was an Aberdeen lad who'd come to London to meet some Spurs mates and see them play the following day. Fair enough I thought but was then thinking how I could get myself out of a situation where people were expecting me to do something when he volunteered that he was on his way to St Pancras because he wanted to see the place where QPR had ambushed Luton in the 80's. The row had been captured on CCTV and was made famous by a documentary at the time. It was just before my time on the scene but I never knew that it was part of some kind of hooligan history trail. I didn't know how it started and didn't really care but his asking them for directions seemed to be the trigger. When I told him that I was QPR and what had happened earlier on in the day, his face lit up and I thought he was going to ask for my autograph. He went on to say how well respected QPR were up in Aberdeen which surprised me. I wasn't really sure if he was trying to stroke my ego in order to get away but if this was the case then I'd be truly surprised as we barely got any credit outside of West London.

My suspicion that things were going to get worse were confirmed pretty quickly when the headlines in Monday's Evening Standard reported that an incident room had been set up to investigate the trouble. My solicitor as always was on the case trying to find out what he could before I surrendered to bail. He also asked me if I knew a lad called 'Macca' who it appeared was an undercover copper that had managed to embed himself with the Chelsea and Reading lads. The only Macca I was aware of was a weird Irishman that I'd met in London when England was playing. He claimed to be from Belfast but his accent seemed more southern Irish to me, if he was undercover old bill then he was a terrible actor and crap at his job so I dismissed it. Whilst on bail I carried on life as normal but early one morning on my way home from work as I was approaching the Stevenage South junction on the A1M, a dark blue Vauxhall in front of me started to indicate that it would be exiting. It had slowed down way too early and was pissing me off so I put my foot down and overtook it with the intention of exiting at the same junction. As I passed my intention was to catch the drivers' attention and demonstrate my displeasure at his over cautious driving. I drew level and what I saw made me nearly crash my car. I recognized the driver and his two passengers straight away as members of the QPR football intelligence unit. I was so shocked that I missed the junction and headed for the next one. I reached across for my mobile phone and quickly found my solicitors number which I dialled immediately. He didn't answer so I left a message explaining the situation. As I pulled into my close, my parents were just leaving for work, I waved to them and did a quick scan for the Vauxhall but it wasn't there. The thought that my mum and dad could have been present while the house was being searched filled me with dread. My old man would have gone ballistic. My solicitor then rang me and I explained what I'd seen. He figured as I had already surmised that they would be coming round to execute a search warrant because if they wanted to arrest me again they would have got the locals to do it. He advised me he knew being a mainly law abiding citizen that they wouldn't find anything incriminating in my house. I agreed but just for safe measure I had a quick check just to be absolutely sure. I remember one time taking part in a massive army exercise in North Carolina. During a bit of R & R myself and a few fellow Paratroopers were amazed at the variety of weaponry freely on sale to the American public. Now my memory is a bit hazy here, probably due to the ridiculous amount of jumps we did in such a short time but I seem to vaguely remember that a seventy thousand volt stun gun and pepper spray was purchased. I can't remember who it was but anyone caught with such items could end up in jail for possessing them, thankfully there was nothing like that in my house at the time of the search. When the knock on the door came, I was actually very surprised because from the moment I had spotted them to the time they arrived was about two hours and I was starting to question whether I had seen what I had. My brother and sister were just leaving for school and I instructed them to say I wasn't in. I think my visitors almost bought it but one of them came in and walked around the downstairs and found me crouched by the fridge. They explained why they were there and said I'd only be arrested if they found anything significant. I took them to my bedroom where they took the clothes I wore on the day and a stack of football hooligan books. In one of my cupboards where I kept my old military kit an officer PC JS found two lumps of metal. I said I didn't know what they were when asked but I was informed that they were gas parts from a SA80 assault rifle. It was just my luck that PC S was also ex army and although he agreed though that all good soldiers carried a spare set of gas parts, he wouldn't be drawn on whether he had done so too during his time. There must have been doubt in his mind though because I didn't get arrested for them and they left with the clothes, books and 'gas parts'. I then went to bed.

When the day came to surrender to bail I had a good idea of what to expect. I had spoken quite a lot to Dave C who had been one of the mad men fighting on the terracing. He'd been through a bit of an ordeal having also been nicked and after his interview he had been charged with conspiracy to commit violent disorder and remanded to Wandsworth. The same thing had happened to Mark G and he was to remain there as he couldn't get the surety to gain his freedom. Dave told me that the detective sergeant running the show was a right horrible bastard so I really did fear the worst. When I met with Danny my solicitor he informed me that the police had CCTV footage of the events but for the time being were only going to show still photos. He advised me to make a statement to the effect that as they (the police) were only prepared to show still images that no adverse inference could be drawn from my no comment to any questioning. My first impression of the DS was that Dave was definitely right about him and that was about as good as it got. He was a horrible sneering bastard who had the kind of face that needs a good slap. The first thing he did was to produce the alleged SA80 gas parts and ask me what they were. Danny interjected and said that to him they looked like lumps of metal, he stated that they were parts of a weapon and arrested me there and then for possessing them. Wandsworth here I come, I thought to myself. He then moved on to the events at Craven Cottage producing his photographs and making comments. One picture showed a woman with an outstretched arm. He tried to make out that she was protecting a child from me but the reality was that she was the one who tripped me up causing me to receive a bit of a hiding. At one point in the interview the DS called me a thug, Danny countered him saying that he was airing an opinion. This seemed to incense the detective sergeant and he shot back that I was a thug. We were all thugs according to him. I just sat there thinking bloody hell he's saying all this and it's all being recorded on tape, perhaps he isn't so bad after all. Once the interview was over I could tell he wasn't happy and he just stormed off without even saying goodbye. I was led to the custody area where I was charged by one of the QPR football coppers with the same offence as Dave C. I later found out that Mark G and MM were also facing the same charges. I went to the pub with Danny where we discussed the case. I wished I shared his confidence that the police had nothing but the whole situation just didn't feel right to me, I felt that we were all being stitched up. I asked Danny what sort of sentence I could get if convicted and he just laughed that any offence with conspiracy attached to it carries a maximum of life. I didn't hear the part where he went on to state, but you would never get that for this. Before Danny and I went our separate ways he again asked me about the mysterious 'Macca'. I could only repeat what I had said before that I wasn't sure I knew him and I also couldn't picture what he looked like.

Before I appeared in court Danny called me with news on Macca. It turned out he wasn't an undercover copper, it was worse, he was revealed to be a BBC journalist called Donal MacIntyre. It turned out he had hours of covert film footage and his documentary was about to be broadcast the following month just before my first court appearance. The conspiracy charge had me worried but when this bombshell dropped, I can honestly say that for the first time I was shitting myself. I had been involved in quite a lot with the Chelsea boys and the time I first became aware of Macca was at an England game and we had got up to all sorts of mischief that day. I really didn't need this and when 'Macintyre Undercover' aired, I avidly watched it, not for any kind of gratification but to see if I featured in it. When the credits rolled I was a relieved man but had an ominous feeling that the main protagonists Andy F, Jason M and my good mate Danny W would soon have the law bearing down on them. This proved to be the case with Andy and Jason both being investigated by the kindly DS and his team, and subsequently convicted.

One of the great things about the firm of solicitors that we chose to represent us was that even if you were only appearing in magistrate's court they would try and supply you with a barrister. Barristers usually advocate in crown courts but when they work in the magistrates they tend to run rings around prosecutors and it is a joy to watch them demolish prosecutors and clerks of the court. I met my barrister for the day, Robert in the waiting area at West London Magistrates court in Hammersmith. He took me into a room where we discussed the case. The first thing he informed me of though was that the conspiracy to commit violent disorder charge had been dropped to section 4 of the public order act. I couldn't believe it and from that moment on, I couldn't have cared less what the final outcome would be. He went on to tell me that from the evidence he had seen that the case for the crown was at best flimsy and if I fought it I would have an excellent chance of winning, even in the magistrates court where the burden of proof is lower. As we sat talking, the room we were in was practically like an open plan office with high thin walls that didn't fully extend to the ceiling meaning that you could easily hear the conversations in adjoining partitions. In the room next to us counsel was discussing with his client his soon to be heard charge of indecent exposure. He went on to document his extensive record of similar type offences up and down the country and seemingly soft sentences. Now on the one hand these rooms offered no confidentiality whatsoever which is not good but on the other it highlighted the fact that I was in the vicinity of a nonce who the courts appeared to keep giving second chances to. When I left our room he came out at the same time and clapped eyes on him, I was shocked to see that he looked like just a normal respectable bloke which probably made him all the more dangerous. I often wonder if his appearance that day would've been his last. I somehow doubt it was, and like most nonces he has probably graduated to a more severe offending pattern which is a damning indictment on our justice system, that appears to view fighting at a football match as more serious than sexually motivated offending. I don't know what happened to the flasher but my appearance in front of the magistrates was uneventful and I was re-bailed to appear again at a later stage to set a date for trial on the lesser charge.

When I did next appear in court I arranged to meet with Dave C and we met also met up with MM. Once we were sat in the dock a door opened behind us and in walked Mark G who was still on remand. By now all defendants had been supplied with the video of the events and from my point of view it totally corroborated my version of events. The prosecution case against me was a joke but the person I really felt sorry for was Mark G. There was nothing on him and he had been held on remand for ages, for me he was purely being punished for his notoriety on the London football scene and it was no surprise when the stipendiary magistrate granted him bail. The prosecution even tried to oppose this. The trial date was set and the three of us who walked in, left as four.

The venue for the trial was switched from West London to Marylebone magistrates ,which did worry me slightly and caused me to question whether the prosecution were trying to stack the odds in their favour by switching to a more favourable venue. I once faced an affray charge at Blackfriars only for it to be switched at the last minute to Southwark Crown court. I won that one so reasoned that if I did it then, I could do it again. All four of us had pleaded not guilty but at the last minute both Dave and MM changed to guilty. I thought this wise especially in the magistrate's court where trying to explain fighting with opposition fans when in their end would be a tall order. If it was in front of a jury then they did stand a good chance. I faced the magistrate alone and listened to the prosecutor try to explain how I was the aggressor, despite the CCTV evidence showing me trying to get away, being easily restrained by the police and then being punched in the head whilst restrained. This had all been documented in the police transcripts and even the Fulham lad who sucker punched me was named in it. Turned out he was one of their top chaps, so fair one I suppose. Not that I would have pursued it any further but I hadn't even been asked about this assault on me, which just confirmed in my mind that this was a total hatchet job. The magistrate for her part said she believed there was more to my situation but the crown had failed to prove on the balance of probability that I was guilty. Case dismissed. I didn't really care if I was found guilty or not as I knew that the worst I would probably get is a big fine and possibly community service with a ban thrown in for good measure. I went back to the pub and waited for Dave C and MM to receive their punishments. I was pretty sure that they'd both be OK but the nice old almost grandmotherly magistrate apparently flipped into wicked witch mode when she read their extensive lists of football related convictions. She threw the book at them and they both narrowly avoided jail terms.

Although I walked away scot free the whole episode had been a massive wake up call for me. When I analyzed all that had gone on – getting a kicking, arrested for affray, the early morning knock, getting charged with conspiracy to commit violent disorder, Donal bloody Macintyre, a serial nonce walking free, I had to question how bent the system was with regards to football and if it was all worth risking my liberty over. I reasoned that it would probably be best for me to take a voluntary break.

About a year later I came across a newspaper report detailing the arrest and investigation of two police officers, one of whom was PC JS. He had been present at my initial arrest and was also a part of the search team. He along with another officer had been investigated by a police anti-corruption unit for aggravated burglary where a noxious substance had been sprayed and he had further been arrested for possession of cannabis and the theft of a police computer. When I told the lads we all decided it would be fun to witness his upcoming appearance at Bow Street magistrates. Perhaps we could offer some practical legal advice? When he saw us, he tried to laugh it off and put on a brave face but it didn't wash with us and we could see he was not only shitting himself but also deeply embarrassed. To be fair though we went there to gloat but when it came down to it, we were better than that and let it slide. He and his co-accused went all the way to trial and were eventually acquitted however he faced a professional misconduct hearing with the Met, probably for the theft allegation and cannabis possession, I didn't know what the outcome of that was but surprisingly despite all that gone on, I didn't bear him any ill will.

8 BANNED

I had been banned from football in 1989 for a stupid incident with some Derby fans at home, I was pissed as usual and tried to get on their coach and was hastily nicked! I received an eighteen month banning order and a six week spell in the slammer.

This was the era when a lot of my mates and a lot of lads at football started to get into the acid house and rave scene. I was living with a very well known Chelsea face, famed for being banged up thanks to the McIntyre Uncovered documentary on TV. Jason was getting into the scene as well and I just couldn't get my head round all the loved up mentality. I did start to like the music though and I started to get right on the speed. I was in a right mess and I was now hanging round with an old mate. We got banged up for a shop burglary and I had another charge of Affray for a row in a pub in Richmond. I got 18 months and served 13 of those and I ended up in Camp Hill prison on the Isle of Wight.

My first ban for that Derby match hardly affected my football as I was in nick for most of it!

When I came out in early 1991 I did start to get into the E's and the rave scene myself. I did not go to football that much as I was more interested in doing all dayers on the piss after a Friday night on the jack and jills in a good club or two.

As I have described in the previous chapter I was banned again in 2000 for the Fulham incident. It was in that year that I left my first wife and went on a mad self-destruct mission on the booze and necking E's like smarties, I was totally off my nut.

I tried to stay away from football as much as I could, my banning order from the Fulham game did not include having to stay away from the grounds within a certain distance. So I still went to meet the lads on occasion just for the piss up and laughs.

In those early 2000's there had been some incidents with some surprise teams at home. One was when a load of Mansfield fans had got into one of our pubs The Adelaide. That had kicked off and also Colchester had bought a good mob although not a lot had happened.

Brentford away in 2001 was a big one, when a load of QPR went back after the game and smashed up a couple of their pubs.

Things were still going on and I was keeping well out of it, until my ban finally came to an end in 2001. My first game back I met the lads in a pub down the Goldhawk Road and got on the coach to Crewe away. I mugged myself off, I had been on the sniff the night before and was spiralling out of control on the booze. I got nicked before I even entered the ground for my first game back. So that was another three year ban which would take me up to 2004.

It was a pre-season friendly against Ajax at home and finally I was allowed back in. But oh no I had to sabotage it all again by getting nicked for fronting a load of Dutch lads as they were giving it the big one coming down the South Africa Road near the ground.

I was getting bad back on the E's and booze and I had left my first wife. It was like I was on self a destruct mission.

Ban number four then took me to the year 2007. I officially retired from any further trouble back in 2004 and also gave up the booze and all other substances. Hey presto, I have never been nicked again, there must have been a common denominator, Booze + Football = trouble!

I had to miss some great games in QPR's history due to those bans, the play off final with Cardiff, the pre-season tournament in Ibiza where it all kicked off with Coventry on a grand scale. I also missed out on our promotion winning match at Hillsborough v Sheffield Wednesday when we took about eight thousand fans up there.

Hey ho that is the consequences of getting involved, I had now had enough and with my new found sobriety I started to change my attitude.

There was a big test of my character though when we played Swansea, Cardiff and Millwall at home in 2010. Miraculously I managed to not get involved.

Here are some write ups about the Swansea game;

Swansea Home. March 2010.

Violence broke out following Swansea City's Championship clash with Queens Park Rangers on Saturday evening. Police were forced to intervene as up to a hundred fans clashed outside Loftus Road in London's Shepherds Bush.

It is understood that between fifty and a hundred fans were led away by officers outside the ground. A spokesman for London Metropolitan Police said: "A disturbance occurred outside the ground at approximately 5pm between supporters from both clubs. Officers moved quickly to diffuse the situation and escorted the Swansea fans away from the conflict."

One eyewitness said: "As we left the stadium the police led us up a road and past a local pub called the Springbok where the trouble started.

"There seemed to be a skirmish.

"You could see glasses being thrown but police reacted very quickly.

"There was another scuffle outside White City tube station later on."

Trouble spilled into the streets after Swansea fans were left frustrated inside the ground as their Championship game finished one apiece.

However, police were unable to confirm whether there had been any arrests.

Swans manager Paulo Sousa, returning to West London for the first time since he was sacked by QPR in April last year, had criticized Rangers boss Neil Warnock's physical approach to games in the build-up. And Warnock, speaking after the game, made his own dig at Swansea.

He said: "I did tell the players not to tackle today so as not to upset Paulo."

Meanwhile, on social networking website Twitter, some QPR fans have hit out at the behaviour of Swansea supporters. Sonnypike posted: "Swansea fans starting a fight with a police horse. A special kind of class."

And another Twitter post from ukcomic said: "Just had to run with my 10-year-old to get out of a fight between Swansea City and QPR supporters.

"It was like the 1970s again." from "This is South Wales"

"Fulham Chronicle"

Rampaging football thugs forced families to run to safety after violent clashes broke out near Loftus Road last weekend. Witnesses reported seeing up to 100 QPR and Swansea fans fighting pitched battles outside The Springbok bar in South Africa Road after the final whistle last Saturday.

Police struggled to contain the warring supporters, who hurled bottles at each other and even attacked a police horse.

Terrified bystanders compared the violence to that of the 1970s, a notorious era for football-related hooliganism.

The Springbok's licensee, TM, was forced to close her doors and said the level of violence was unprecedented in the two years she has run the bar.

She accused police of being under prepared for the visit of the Welsh club's notorious fans, and has also blamed the QPR for serving them alcohol during the match.

She said: "Some of the Swansea fans who came in here before the violence kicked off said Loftus Road was only the third ground in the country where they'd been allowed to drink. There should have been a ban.

"There was a lot of trouble and not enough police there. There were only four wagons and by the time they got here it had already started.

"People were getting hit with batons and I saw a QPR fan go for a horse. I have never really ever seen a fight since I've been here but I know there has been trouble with Swansea in the past.

"Thank God there wasn't more serious injuries. But I'm worried about Cardiff coming down here now, this is just going to make things worse and they need to make the kick-off earlier."

Cardiff fans contributed to violence in Fulham Broadway following an FA Cup match with Chelsea last month.

A QPR spokesman defended the club's policy of serving alcohol during the match, saying: "The issue was not the amount that they were drinking in the stadium. We didn't serve those that we believe had been drinking throughout the day.

"For the record, we declined entry to a number of those

that were drunk on arrival and some supporters were also ejected during the match."

Police said three arrests were made for public order offences and said about forty people were fighting. A spokesman said: "Officers moved quickly to diffuse the situation."

Millwall home. Millwall had made it very clear they were coming in force to avenge the incident that took place at Baker Street when they came a bit unstuck. And one thing is certain with Millwall is they will always come back and bite harder!

I was working in Ealing at the time and every man and his dog had arranged to meet early doors to protect the British Queen pub, who Millwall said they were going to take over. It is believed that a hardcore of about twenty Wall came early and as they passed the Crown and Sceptre pub down the backstreets an off occurred with a small group of QPR and a few Spurs youth who had come along for the fun.

As the Wall lot got nearer the Queen pub a load of ours had come out to confront them and old bill were all over it like a rash. That was the end of that.

A mate of mine had got me a ticket for the game and he was in the Queen and all the lads in there, at least two hundred or more were now locked in and kettled by the police. I was unable to get away from work early and missed it all, and as I came down by the 207 bus the whole of the Uxbridge Road near the Bush was at a standstill. It looked like something serious had happened and I have never seen so many old bill vans lined up at a game before or since. Except for when we have played Millwall again!

As I went to enter the pub, the ring of old bill told me that if I went in there I would not be coming back out. I asked could I get my ticket off my mate, I was denied this and had to hope my pal could get the ticket to me in time for kick off.

The QPR lads in there tried breaking out like the great escape but were totally hemmed in.

Meanwhile down the other end at the Green, Millwall had massed and they must have had a good mob of five hundred or so that was escorted to the ground. There would have been absolute carnage if the two firms had met before the game.

The police waited until they got all of the Millwall escort in the ground before letting the lads out of the Queen pub. They didn't make it to the ground until half time. So I missed the first half, it was a shit match anyway.

After the game everyone was mobbing up and I literally had to pull myself away and go straight home as I did not want to get nicked again.

I heard all about when I phoned my mates the next day, it had been very interesting indeed.

This is what the press said;

Riots in Shepherd's Bush after QPR v Milwall.

Rioting football thugs brought bedlam to the streets of Shepherd's Bush on a night of shameful violence on Tuesday. There were reports of major disorder before, during and after the match between QPR and Millwall, with rival fans engaging in violent clashes along Wood Lane, Uxbridge Road and near Westfield Shopping Centre. There are as yet unconfirmed reports that a supporter was stabbed in a pub prior to the match, which finished 0-0.

By 11pm police had confirmed they had arrested 11 people

for a variety of offences including possessing an offensive weapon, common assault, assaulting police and affray.

They could not confirm how many from each club had been detained. Fans and witnesses besieged social networking site Twitter and variously described the area around Loftus Road as a 'war zone', 'bedlam' and 'like being back in the 1970s', with many R's fans accusing Millwall supporters of behaving like 'animals'.

Some said they saw some of the Bermondsey team's fans hitting women and children and there were also reports of a QPR fan with two darts sticking from his chest. Seats were ripped and coins thrown during the game, according to some fans.

Other supporters said Millwall fans stormed at the home crowd after the final whistle, with some criticizing police for not keeping visiting fans in the ground after full-time. A massive police presence descended on W12 before the game, with dogs, horses, riot officers and helicopters deployed to deal with the south London team's notoriously hardcore following.

A video posted on Twitter showed trouble brewing about an

hour-and-a-half before kick-off, as a large number of Millwall fans arrived in Shepherd's Bush Green.

Police confirmed there was disorder before the match in the Walkabout bar (Millwall fans) and The British Queen (QPR fans), while Shepherd's Bush blogger Chris Underwood was caught up in violence at The Conningham Arms.

He said fans were kept in the pub by police to prevent them clashing with Millwall supporters but that things turned nasty when some R's fans tried to breech the police line, resulting in many fans arriving late at the game. Mr Underwood said QPR fans had behaved as badly as their Millwall counterparts prior to the match. "Mylondon.news"

In July 2017 QPR played away at Union Berlin for a pre-season friendly. I personally have never travelled abroad to see the R's play, something I hopefully will get to do one day.

We took a good amount of supporters out there, the first game was abandoned due to torrential rain. The day the game went ahead a load of our loyal travelling lads were having a good old jolly up in a pub and it was attacked by a firm of hooded Union fans. The lads held their own which they had to do really in self defense. A few had to appear later back in court, which I believe went well as justice went their way. The Germans also had taken a QPR flag, something that the continentals deem as a "result".

The following season, Union Berlin was invited back to Loftus Road for a return friendly. Fair play they bought two thousand passionate fans and apparently made a lot of noise. After the game when they were escorted past the Springbok pub, they were taunting some of the lads with the robbed flag. Let's just say the flag was returned to the rightful owners!

9 YOUTH

Back in the 1980's I was a teenager and loved mixing it with the older lads especially the C-Mob. There was no particular divide back then as we all mixed together. Although West Ham and the ICF had their own youth branch known as the "Under Fives". In the late 1990's QPR formed a youth mob, one of the lads has written the following accounts for this book and wishes to be known as "DK";

Saturday 28th December 1998

Barnsley v QPR

"The Birth & Death of the Gap Band"

At the age of sixteen I was in full swing of being allowed to travel up and down the country with mates following our beloved QPR. We were very much what you say as 'active' then, from getting numbers from other teams off the Paul Dodd website, or swapping numbers with other youth firms to arrange meets whoever we had at the weekend. We had quite a name for ourselves with other clubs but no one really knew us at QPR. This had to change, we needed something to 'put us on the map' with our own lot. We didn't look the part as most of us were still in the final year of high school or in college with apprenticeships, so Stone Island and Aquascutum wasn't quite in our reach just yet. Back then the trend for our age group was the GAP hoodie. Everyone in our group had one, so I came up with the idea that we all will wear one to an away game.

The meeting place for the boys was Euston Station at 07:45 ready for the 08:15 train to Barnsley. Some had bought train tickets, most didn't, the ones that's didn't all piled into the toilet cubicle when the inspector past through. So the lads and myself got up to our usual tricks to pass the time getting to our destination, this included breaking into the bar and tea leafing all the miniature bottle of spirits and cans of beer etc.

Arriving into Barnsley I can honestly say I've never had so

many confused looks as I had that day, fifteen to twenty youths being escorted to the ground all wearing GAP jumpers. Walking into the away end we were also laughed at by our own supporters. I couldn't believe it, it was the opposite of what we wanted for an outcome. But with us lot sitting at the front giving as much grief and abuse as possible to the home end as well as the old bill for the whole ninety minutes. The Jeers soon turned to cheers from the Rangers loyal!

One of our lot pushed it a bit far and got nicked inside the ground, even tough it meant we were going to miss our train home we wasn't going to leave him there so we all agreed to wait for him at the plod Shop until they let him go. Someone on the QPR LSA coach caught wind of this and offered to wait for us so we can jump on the coach back. I knew right then it would be full of absolute diamonds on there. So he got released and we all bundled on to the coach, we were the focus of all the blokes jokes on there, mainly due to the fact that GAP had a Christmas advert out at the time so they all kept singing the jingle to mug us of, but we didn't care.

We lost the game that day 1-0 but for me I won a whole lot

more. I won my first experience of the QPR LSA Party Bus and we set out what we achieved to do that day as well. Even though that was the first and last time we all wore the same jumpers to a match, but what's more, is that I got to know fellas on there that became brothers over the years, and are my best of mates to this very day!

The following are from "Original Yoof"

Ibiza football tournament 2005; QPR , Coventry, Huddersfield, Ibiza XI

What a time to be alive!

Towards the end of the season there were lots of rumours about a tournament in Ibiza with other English clubs. This seemed too good to be true QPR playing in a tournament in Ibiza bang in the middle of summer.

The rumours then became reality. QPR had been invited to Ibiza to play in a tournament along side Coventry and Huddersfield, every man and his dog was saying they was going and there wasn't much time from the announcement to the start of the tournament. Us yoof all booked up to go with big numbers plus a big firm of the older lads. As the weeks went by the excitement was building for everyone.

QPR, sun, beer, Ibiza!

The day had arrived and the phone non stopped ringing all morning. This was a dream away trip and the closest I will ever get to watching QPR in Europe. Arriving at the airport to meet all the other yoof lads everyone was buzzing and beers were opened and packets opened.

All the older lads had travelled a day or two before hand and we were hearing the story's that it had been kicking off already. We couldn't wait to get on the plane and land in Ibiza. Once we were on the plane there was actually an announcement saying that Ibiza have had to draft in extra police from Barcelona due to a football tournament and to stay safe. This week was probably a bad idea to have a booked a nice week away with your Missus to Ibiza.

Once we landed at the hotel and a quick change and out and get right amongst it. We knew Huddersfield and Coventry had both brought big numbers. We went straight to meet the older lads in a bar which believe it or not was called the orange bar. This was now our strong hold. We heard the night before that it was kicking off with Coventry lads in the main strip. So we were looking forward to the night ahead. During the night everyone seemed to have gone off and done there own things around Ibiza, a few of us was walking up past some bars and had glasses thrown at us and a roar went up it was Coventry lads we were now trading with these Coventry lads and the next thing people were pouring out of the bars and screaming. It was coming on top due to numbers but then we heard another roar go up and it was our lot coming up, this then kicked off before riot police came straight in hitting everyone in sight. This strip was now a like a war zone and the local bar owners were out with bats hitting any English they could see. I got straight in a taxi back to the hotel to get away from being nicked. Now this was the first twenty four hours and we have had a riot in the middle of the strip of Ibiza causing it to close down for the night. The next day it seemed all our lads had some sort of trouble with Coventry or Huddersfield the night before. We had missed the game with Coventry as it was played before we had arrived in Ibiza. But we were now playing Coventry in the final in the Ibiza stadium. We all met up and walked up to the ground about a hundred of us and we didn't see any Coventry en route walking up to the ground. This will stay with me forever it is not everyday you are a hundred plus handed walking in an Ibiza street looking for Coventry. Once we made it into the ground we saw Coventry lads were already in the ground in big numbers also. Now this ground was open so we were right next to them with no separation. There was however police around and a few stewards. Within a minute a few of ours walked over to speak to the Coventry lads, punches then started and again it was kicking off in the stadium. The police managed to get in between with big batons they liked using on us. The game had to be stopped due to the trouble and our manager at the time Ian Holloway came on the mike and was begging us to stop fighting etc so they could finish the game. However we won the game 3-2 and Coventry lads were led out the ground way before us and when we made our way out Coventry were no where to be seen. We went back to the main strip, I remember being in a bar called funky flares and remembered pig bag being played and the gaff went mental. Again there was trouble on the strip, at every corner you turned there were QPR flags or you could hear QPR songs being sung. It was like Shepherds Bush in Ibiza. I had been in Ibiza for three nights so far and all those nights there had been disorder, beer and birds. What a trip so far. As the week went on the trouble did get quieter and we didn't need to go out mob handed, during the day and nights everywhere was just QPR fans. It was a trip that will never happen again and the things that people got up to is unbelievable unless you were there. Getting the whole west end strip locked down and armed police on patrol was madness. I didn't see much of Huddersfield, although Coventry had a good tidy firm and respect to them for going out there too.

Aston Villa away.

This was the third round Carling Cup game and was a midweek 8pm kick-off. Villa at the time was in the Premiership and we were in the Championship. When the draw was made we decided to make the trip and we had a coach organized plus loads had made there own way up via train and cars.

Aston Villa football club wasn't expecting a big crowd and didn't want to pay for the policing. When we landed we went straight to a boozer, we was around eighty handed, five minutes before the end of the game we arranged to all meet in the concourse and all leave together, bearing in mind there was no police. We left the ground and done the right and didn't see any Villa, so we waited on the corner. Both home and away fans were now pouring out of the ground with a few false alarms with the shouts "They are here" and "here they are" but then one of ours then walked over the road and saw them coming. He landed a head butt and then it just kicked off big time, Villa and us were both at it with no police and Villa were scattered. We then re-grouped by the coach park opposite the ground and then there were loads of stewards in a big line separating Villa and us, Villa had also regrouped and were pushing through the stewards line and were getting banged, the line was broken in seconds and was again a free for all. They couldn't live with us what we had that night. Once it all ended we jumped back on the coach and as we were leaving a few windows got put through with bricks, we emptied the coach and Villa ran again. We got back on the coach for a cold journey back home.

Millwall away.

A few seasons back we decided to hatch a plan to land in Surrey Quays without any old bill. The plan was to meet in a certain boozer then leave later on than all the shirters. The plan worked great as we were on the train we pulled into London Bridge. There were no police as the main big crowd was on the few trains before hand so the old bill took them all off and was escorting them to the ground. When we first got on the train we were about fifty handed and as the train pulled into London Bridge there was a lot of "I need to go get my ticket", "I need to meet so and so" so our numbers had dwindled to about twenty by the time we pulled into Surrey Quays. This was now stupid we had twenty of us bang in Surrey Quays with no old bill and we knew Millwall were out big for us in Surrey Quays we did have a good game twenty with top faces with us. We came to a little boozer with a couple of dressers outside smoking. They looked shocked and said who are you we said we are QPR!!

One of our older lads said we are not bullies so phone your lot and tell them we are here (I was thinking fuck sake don't do that) but we then carried on walking up the road near some park when I looked back the fella outside was straight on his phone (obviously calling the Millwall lot and telling them we are here). As we were walking up the road I was thinking any minute Millwall will start appearing. A riot van pulled up besides us and the football intelligence officer jumped out and straight away called for back up, I said to him we are just walking to the ground and he said the back up wasn't for us but for what's coming through the park. The roar went up and Millwall were coming through the park, there were loads and loads of them. More police arrived and we were then escorted to the ground. I am not sure if that was a blessing or not getting wrapped up in Surrey Quays twenty handed with a pub load of Millwall two minutes away.

Sheffield Wednesday away.

Yoof made the trip to this one. We organized to get a coach but when the morning came the coach driver wouldn't let us on with crates of beer. No way were we going to travel three and a half hours with no beer. So fifteen or so of us jumped off and made our way to Kings Cross and caught the train up instead. When we arrived in Sheffield we caught the tram link which took us to the ground. As we were approaching some random stop, I saw lads all piling out of this boozer and came running over pulling there hoods up. To be honest they had big numbers and most were meat heads. As soon as the tram doors opened it was on top straight away. We stayed tight and gave as good as we got until old bill arrived. We then got wrapped up. After the game we were waiting for the tram and loads and loads of Wednesday lads were mixed in with us. There were loads of old bill around with us too, but they didn't click on at this point. One of their lads said to me to get on the next tram and we will get on with you and the old bill won't get on.

It did make sense why they didn't kick off with us there and then plus old bill was all around too. As the tram was pulling in their football intelligence officer started pointed out their lads and stopped them getting on the tram with us. Hats off to the Wednesday lads it was a great idea but didn't work which was probably good for us fifteen though haha.

West Brom away.

This was another great away day out. The day started as every away day starts, up early and then meet the lads at the station then straight on the beers. About twenty five of us made the trip and we arrived at their station early and made our way to a boozer not far from the ground. The boozer was called the Coach and Horses, this boozer was a strange boozer as beer was being poured into plastic cups from warm beer cans. I am not even sure if they had electricity in there.

We were plotted up in the beer garden enjoying our warm beer and a few of our lads had just also come off their bans. Around 1pm- ish a couple of the young lads with us came running in the beer garden shouting "They're here, they're here" We poured out of the beer garden which brought us out onto a road and West Brom were there bouncing about with around the same numbers. It then kicked off proper toe to toe with no one moving. It was game lads on both sides. The old bill then quickly arrived and it was all ended. There were around twelve nicked. That was a proper toe to toe and massive respect to West Brom for that.

Nottingham Forest away.

This was probably one of the best firms I've seen from QPR on an away day where there was top old school faces. We landed in Nottingham around 10am and I genuinely believe we could of took this firm anywhere in the country and hold our own. We did think as we landed so early that we wouldn't get wrapped up but when we pulled into Nottingham we were greeted by Nottinghamshire police with dogs. We was then escorted to a boozer with the old bill being heavy handed along the way being trigger happy with there coshes. That was end of that day, the old bill had us under wraps.

QPR Christmas party –Millwall.

We always meet up for a Christmas beer and we decided to

travel up to Paddington for this occasion. The boozer was a nice back street boozer and the beers were flowing and we were having a great afternoon. Millwall were travelling back from an away game up North and would be pulling into Paddington. What we had in this boozer was the proper A-team, no idiots and Millwall would have there hands full if they did land. We thought Millwall may have been wrapped up or wouldn't appear. Lo and behold Millwall turned up outside the pub forty odd handed with hoods on and bouncing shouting "come on QPR". We steamed out of the pub, Millwall then ran straight away leaving a few of theirs to get a pasting. We chased them around Paddington. Now in my opinion Millwall are a top firm and they thought they could land on us and take the piss but on this occasion it didn't work. Landing at a boozer full of top table QPR lads was never going to go to plan for them. Since then Millwall have come to us every game with hundreds.

Bristol City away.

This was another early start and I believe this was first game of the season. At the station we had a massive firm of young and old, it was bang in the middle of summer. This one stands out to me as the escort to the ground was about a ten mile walk in the blazing heat. We had made ourselves known before the game. During the game both sets had tried to get to each other and few arrests were made. After the game we didn't have an escort to start with and a load of us had made our way out away from the old bill and we found ourselves on a main road and saw some Bristol lads next to a subway. We went over and had a bit of toe to toe with them, then old bill on horses and foot managed to get in between and then we was wrapped up and escorted once again back to the station. This again felt like a two hour walk with the sun beating down on us with no beer.

On route back to the station Bristol had got it together now and was making the effort to try and break the escort coming through a park at us. This was another great away day.

Watford away.

This was the worst away day for me personally. We arranged to land at Watford's main pub fifteen handed early doors at 11 am. We personally wasn't expecting what we found at 11am when it was absolutely rammed with lads. They obviously were told our plan. As we turned the corner towards the pub they emptied on us with everything in the pub from plant pots to pool cues and glasses etc. It is safe to say we got turned over and was a complete piss take and one lesson learned from it was never to under estimate any firm.

Fulham away (night game).

We don't normally nowadays really turn out in a big mob for Fulham. But this game we decided to go over and make some noise. We knew we would be wrapped up going into Hammersmith or going by train so we decided to meet in a boozer out of the way in Shepherd's Bush and we then got taxis straight over the water to a back street boozer in Putney. We then made moves in ones and twos and met up on a side street with Fulham's pub two minutes around the corner. We then walked out onto the road and could see some of them drinking and smoking outside and as soon as they saw thirty of us walking towards them their pints dropped on the floor. They threw their fags down on the floor and ran inside the pub and locked the doors. We were at the windows telling them to come out and beckoning them out the pub was packed with them but not one of them had bottle to come out and trade. We then walked back up the bridge and found a boozer. All that effort we went through of slipping the old bill and they didn't want to come out and play.

Hull away.

This is another game that stands out as Hull fans were singing "You're just a town full of bombers" this was after the terrorist attacks in London.

We had a good mob going up on the train and also had a mini bus and coach of lads. After the game we came out and tried to break the metal fence that was separating us from the Hull lads. A few QPR lads managed to get through and end up in a massive car park and it was kicking off. QPR then finally pushed through and the Hull lads eventually got run through the cars after a good kick off. A Hull lad then was on his phone shouting down it to get everyone out the pub to the car park as QPR are here. We were waiting around and no mob came and then we was wrapped up and escorted back to the station.

These away games stand out for all different reasons. Give me an away day over a home game, there is nothing better than an early start landing in a different town or city with your boys.

Cheers. Original yoof.

10 WHY?

Back in the late 1970's and 1980's hooliganism at football matches was a weekly thing for a lot of young men.

Violence at football has been eradicated by the police and authorities very successfully these days. However there are still a very small minority that try and get involved.

Most trouble is more of a sporadic thing these days and is nowhere near on a large scale as it used to be.

Is there any rhyme or reason for the trouble? Who knows; I kind of know the factors behind why I used to get involved.

A sense of belonging

My own anger issues

addictive nature

Intoxication of alcohol and/or substances

Adrenaline rush

I was an angry young man who witnessed and suffered violence from my mother, it was a learned behaviour to be violent.

From an early age I used substances and alcohol and by my own admissions I was an alcoholic with an addictive personality.

My inhibitions were affected by my alcohol use and I used to get a high from the sense of danger and excitement from being involved in fist fights with other football supporters.

"Belonging" to a mob or firm had that sense of belonging and being a "somebody". The human race has always had clans or gangs and to some extent involves a sense of power for each individual and gang.

With any kind of addiction negative consequences arise. And anyone that is addicted always seem to deny those consequences until it is too late. But then there is that masochistic kind of pleasure a bit like extreme sports and the highs associated with them.

I created a poll on a facebook group for lads who were casuals back in the day. I asked what were the reasons you got involved in trouble at football?

A huge percentage of lads say they got involved for the "Buzz" and the second most popular answer was the "sense of belonging". Another reason was that a lot of lads started to get into the casual scene and wearing all the clobber. This just led to being in a gang or firm and just fell in to the violence side of things.

I could relate to the film "Fight Club" which is about a man who suffers from insomnia and his totally unhappy with his life. He asked a friend to hit him as hard as he could as a masochistic act. This made him feel better and that is when he formed a "fight club". So in way the club helped the average Joe feel like they were "somebody" as I have already mentioned.

When I got sober I started to volunteer in a substance misuse service. I then became qualified as a drug and alcohol professional and also gained a counselling qualification. I did that job for seven years and trust me some of the tragedy I heard from alcoholics and addicts was unreal.

Football violence in my opinion is a form of addictive behaviour, just like any addiction it carries negative consequences. Yet people still engage in the behaviour as the "buzz" or high outweighs the bad side to it. It is illogical to the majority of people, but it definitely goes deeper.

In February 2014, there was disorder between QPR and Burnley fans in Hammersmith, four R's fans received between 30 months and a year prison and all banned for six years from football.

In August 2015 the day I got married, there was a big fight at a pub in Bishopsgate, City of London. This was following QPR's first game of the season at Charlton. A lot of the lads went on the piss after and ended up in the city. A pub full of Leyton Orient fans wound them up about our relegation the previous season and it all kicked off.

Twelve QPR fans appeared in court and got prison sentences ranging from ten months to six years.

In September 2013 a QPR fan was jailed for five years and banned for eight years for stabbing an Everton fan outside

Goodison Park during a mild altercation between rival supporters.

The worse aspect of trouble at football both inside and outside the grounds is that innocent people including women and kids have to witness the events. It is scary for them and when I look back on those days in the 1980's and up until I sorted my life out in 2004 I can honestly say it was crazy behaviour.

I took up boxing at the age of fifty which is a much better outlet for having a fight in a controlled manor. More boxing and martial arts clubs would definitely benefit the community.

I now live in Ireland to be near my wife's family, it is so peaceful and a far cry from good old London town. I do miss certain things about city life and I miss my mates and all the lads at QPR. I will get back over there, and hopefully this covid malarkey will be over soon enough.

The last game I went to was Luton at home, there was a massive turnout from us , both old and young. It was like a reunion of old faces and the youth were getting very excited. Fair play to the old bill these days, they have almost everything sussed.

I reckon most lads who were in the scene back in the 80's will still have those days in their blood. Those days can never be relived, they are only memories, just like 80's music time has moved on.

Young men especially in London and the big cities seem to have little respect for their elders now, although that is a bit different at football.

It was about mutual respect really unless you were one of those individuals that bears resentment and grudges. For fuck sake football is only a game after all. When I really try and dig deep inside of me and honestly analyze why I got so het up about rival fans. As I mentioned before, I am sure it is a sense of "false pride" a kind of "how dare they" try and be bigger and better than us!

So it was all about being the better, like a peacock puffing out it's chest and parading it's colourful feathers. Or certain animals that have to take control of their territory, like lions and other species on the African savannahs.

Then there are some guys who do just genuinely like a good scrap, and football hooliganism is an easy way to do this whilst only really affecting those who feel the same.

But i would guess the biggest reason is the 'buzz' you get, every interview I've seen they have mentioned the adrenaline rush you get and how it is very addicting. Makes sense i guess considering many soldiers back this up saying the adrenaline when fighting on the front-line can be addicting, and some soldiers do end up becoming hooligans to try and re-live this buzz. Saw one interview where one bloke was able to give up cocaine but was not able to give up hooliganism, and another where a guy said if he was offered a gorgeous girl or a good football fight he would go with the football fight. I suppose its in a way just a extreme sport, people can get addicted the adrenaline rush it gives.

Everyone that tries to understand how hooliganism works focuses on the fighting and hating the enemy when the majority of it is just about close friendships, trusting your mates and backing each other up no matter what happens.

Like I say it’s only a game, but in the footballing side of things, is it?

The game of football has changed, only this week while I am writing this there was talk of a "Super League". A break-away of the "Big Six".

My first reaction was fuck them, let them go. At least my team QPR might have a better chance to compete again. But then when I thought about it rationally I realized it could be the end of our great game as we know it.

It has been weird without crowds at matches even though I hardly go any more. The first game when a full capacity is allowed back will probably be like another reunion gane. I hope to get over, when I enter the ground it is like I turn into that teenager all over again. There is still that banter between the opposing fans and you can always spot that one loon who is fully charged up among the crowd.

It is about keeping self control although that is not always as easy as it sounds! It sure is easier for me now I am sober and as I approach the age of fifty four I have far too much to lose.

I hope you all enjoyed reading this account of QPR over the years, stay out of trouble and just remember the old days.

ABOUT THE AUTHOR

Dave grew up in London and let's just say his life was "traumatic".
His mother had problems and Dave had no sense of direction.
As a teenager Dave became involved in trouble at his beloved QPR and other criminality due to his own drunkenness.
Due to his chaotic lifestyle Dave ended up in prison several times.
Life certainly was never dull but it also was not the way to go.
After hitting many rock bottoms Dave decided to get sober and even became a qualified counsellor and substance misuse professional himself.
A second marriage followed and then a move to Donegal in Ireland for a more peaceful life.
Dave wrote his memoir "Beating My Demons" describing all the madness and then the recovery .He has now written MemoiR's about supporting QPR with contributions from fellow fans and this latest book about the casual scene and trouble at the games.
"Life's not always easy" Dave admits but it sure is better sober and trying to do the right thing.
Dave shares his experience, strength and hope and wishes for the reader to just to relate to his story.

Printed in Great Britain
by Amazon

64319512R00129